IMAGES OF W

I0893295

THE LIBERATION OF NAZI CONCENTRATION CAMPS

RARE PHOTOGRAPHS FROM WARTIME ARCHIVES

Ian Baxter

Pen & Sword
MILITARY

First published in Great Britain in 2023 by
PEN & SWORD MILITARY
an imprint of Pen & Sword Books Ltd
Yorkshire – Philadelphia

ISBN 978-1-39904-877-4

A CIP catalogue record for this book is available from the British Library.

Typeset by Concept, Huddersfield HD4 5JL.
Printed and bound in England by CPI Group (UK) Ltd, Croydon CR0 4YY.

MIX
Paper | Supporting responsible forestry
FSC® C013604

Pen & Sword Books Limited incorporates the imprints of After the Battle, Atlas, Archaeology, Aviation, Discovery, Family History, Fiction, History, Maritime, Military, Military Classics, Politics, Select, Transport, True Crime, Air World, Frontline Publishing, Leo Cooper, Remember When, Seaforth Publishing, The Praetorian Press, Wharncliffe Local History, Wharncliffe Transport, Wharncliffe True Crime and White Owl.

For a complete list of Pen & Sword titles please contact
PEN & SWORD BOOKS LTD
47 Church Street, Barnsley, South Yorkshire, S70 2AS, England
E-mail: enquiries@pen-and-sword.co.uk
Website: www.pen-and-sword.co.uk
or
PEN & SWORD BOOKS
1950 Lawrence Rd, Havertown, PA 19083, USA
E-mail: uspen-and-sword@casematepublishers.com
Website: www.penandswordbooks.com

Contents

About the Author

Ian Baxter is a military historian who specializes in German twentieth-century military history. He has written more than fifty books including *Poland – The Eighteen Day Victory March, Panzers in North Africa, The Ardennes Offensive, The Western Campaign, The 12th SS Panzer-Division Hitlerjugend, The Waffen-SS on the Western Front, The Waffen-SS on the Eastern Front, The Red Army at Stalingrad, Elite German Forces of World War II, Armoured Warfare, German Tanks of War, Blitzkrieg, Panzer-Divisions at War 1939–1945, Hitler's Panzers, German Armoured Vehicles of World War Two, Last Two Years of the Waffen-SS at War, German Soldier Uniforms and Insignia, German Guns of the Third Reich, Defeat to Retreat: The Last Years of the German Army at War 1943–45, Operation Bagration – the Destruction of Army Group Centre, German Guns of the Third Reich, Rommel and the Afrika Korps, U-Boat War,* and most recently *The Sixth Army and the Road to Stalingrad.* He has written over a hundred articles including 'Last days of Hitler', 'Wolf's Lair', 'The Story of the V1 and V2 Rocket Programme', 'Secret Aircraft of World War Two', 'Rommel at Tobruk', 'Hitler's War With his Generals', 'Secret British Plans to Assassinate Hitler', 'The SS at Arnhem', 'Hitlerjugend', 'Battle of Caen1944', 'Gebirgsjäger at War', 'Panzer Crews', 'Hitlerjugend Guerrillas', 'Last Battles in the East', 'The Battle of Berlin', and many more. He has also reviewed numerous military studies for publication, supplied thousands of photographs and important documents to various publishers and film production companies worldwide, and lectures to various schools, colleges and universities throughout the United Kingdom and Southern Ireland.

Preface

> The things I saw beggar description. The visual evidence and the verbal testimony of starvation, cruelty and bestiality were so overpowering as to leave me a bit sick ... I made the visit deliberately, in order to be in a position to give first-hand evidence of these things if ever, in the future, there develops a tendency to charge these allegations merely to 'propaganda'.
>
> [*General Dwight D. Eisenhower on a visit to Ohrdruf concentration camp, 12 April 1945*]

As the Allies advanced across Europe from the west and the Soviet army advanced from the east at the end of the Second World War, they came across concentration camps filled with dead, sick and starving prisoners.

In this latest of the Images of War series, the book presents a unique visual account of what the soldiers found when they liberated the camps. It also gives the reader a disturbing insight into proof of what the liberators discovered of a brutal regime of murder, torture and starvation.

This book illustrates how the Germans attempted to hide the evidence of mass murder by demolishing much of the camps' infrastructure, including the gas chamber facilities. However, in Poland, the Soviet advance was so rapid that, at the first major camp to be liberated at Majdanek near Lublin, Poland in July 1944, the Germans did not have enough time to destroy their gas chambers and so they were left standing.

As the Red Army pushed forward further into Eastern Europe more camps were unearthed including Auschwitz in January 1945. It was the largest extermination and concentration camp, to which more than 1 million people had been deported from all over Europe. Upon liberation, only a few thousand prisoners remained. Most of the survivors had been taken away on death marches. Many were moved to various other camps including Bergen-Belsen, Buchenwald, Mauthausen, Theresienstadt and Ravensbrück or one of their many sub-camps. The overcrowding in these camps resulted in the spread of disease and caused many more deaths.

In every camp, Allied and Russian soldiers encountered terrible scenes of death and starvation. Bergen-Belsen was another camp liberated by British troops on

15 April 1945. When soldiers walked through the gates, they found approximately 10,000 unburied dead in addition to the mass graves already containing 400,000 more corpses. Nearby in the barracks some 60,000 starving and sick inmates were found packed together without sanitation, food or water.

This book is a compelling account of those who unfortunately perished and those that were fortunate enough to be liberated from a living hell.

Introduction

Concealing Murder

Long before German military reverses, the Nazis had been closing down the apparatus of their heinous crimes. Many of the camps throughout Europe and Russia often operated for months or sometimes weeks before the prisoners inside were evacuated to slave labour or death camps or simply murdered and evidence of the crimes concealed in pits. In 1943 three large camps in Poland, known as the Reinhard camps (from Operation REINHARD), comprising Treblinka, Sobibor and Belzec were closed down and all traces of the Nazis' murderous actions were removed and kept secret. In the eyes of the perpetrators they believed that when the time came and the Allies or Russians arrived to liberate the area, they would not find any trace of the terrible murders inflicted on the people who were sent there. In fact, when the Red Army marched through Treblinka in the summer of 1944 they were told about the murders, the burying of the bodies and the burning of the corpses. When the camp was closed down, gas chambers were removed and transported by rail to Lublin. Other materials including bricks, wood, window frames and roofing were also shipped out by rail. This included furniture and other interior items. Important documents and files, including communiqués, left for Lublin in a convoy of vehicles under armed escort, and anything that was regarded as incriminating evidence was ordered to be burned. Only a handful of SS personnel and Ukrainian guards remained behind in the camp to oversee the dismantling operation. The guards were to ensure that all the corpses were burned to ashes and traces of the crime completely removed.

All remaining SS personnel hitched a lift to Sobibor, while the last train out carried the final pieces of equipment from the camp. What was left in the camp was buried deep in the ground and the only evidence remaining when the last of the personnel departed were traces of barbed wire, heaps of earth and sand, some pits and various pieces of material laying around. A building firm was immediately brought in to construct a farmhouse on top of the existing site using the bricks from the gas chambers. Once this had been hastily built, livestock was brought in and a Ukrainian by the name of Strebel who had been a guard at Treblinka was asked to live there and farm the land with his family. Strebel ensured that no trace of the camp existed and went to work ploughing the land, sowing lupins and planting pine woods where some 800,000 souls had been murdered at the hands of the SS.

The dismantling process at Treblinka was just an example of one camp within the Nazi domain that followed such procedures in order to conceal their murderous activities. As with other camps, much of the main apparatus such as the crematoria and the ovens was dismantled and transported to other camps that were in need of them. In these other installations the killings continued with the systematic annihilation of European Jews until the camps were forced to close as the enemy advanced. Often these camps had time to transport what they called 'livestock' to other camps, but there were many others and various similar installations that had no time to undertake a dismantling process. Instead the prisoners who were too ill or weak to be moved were often either left to die in their barracks or out in the grounds of the camp or were murdered by the guards before they fled. The guards and the SS officers tried to cover up their deeds, endeavouring to make it almost impossible for others to know what they had done. Sometimes the advance of the enemy was so rapid that the concentration camp guards did not have time to flee. Instead they remained in the camp disguised as inmates and sat around piles of malnourished naked corpses or walked among sick and starving prisoners that had had to survive the horrors of the camps. Their disguise was often quickly exposed by the liberators and they were either arrested, shot on the spot or faced angry retribution from the survivors remaining in the camp.

Although the Nazis tried their best to conceal their crimes in the camps, the evidence of what the liberators found when they arrived was overwhelming. The prisoners that survived were the voices of the victims and these survivors live on through their testimony.

Chapter One

Liberation of the Polish Concentration Camps

One of the first main camps to be liberated was Majdanek, constructed on the outskirts of Lublin in Poland. The camp operated from 1 October 1941 to 22 July 1944, and was left almost intact by the SS staff. Due to the rapid advance of the Red Army in the summer of 1944, SS staff at the camp were unable to destroy most of the camp's infrastructure and Deputy Camp Commandant Anton Thernes had no time to order his guards and camp personnel to remove the incriminating evidence of mass murders. When they fled the camp they only managed to partially destroy the crematoria. Most of the records and files were also left behind, leaving a trail of evidence of the murders. On 24 July 1944, Red Army forces arrived in the camp. Although 1,000 of the camp's inmates had been force-marched to Auschwitz, the liberating soldiers still found thousands of surviving inmates in the camp, which allowed the Soviet authorities to prove through the testimonies of the living the mass murders inflicted there.

The soldiers that arrived at the camp were confronted by unimaginable conditions where evidence of half-burned corpses was found and many of the inmates resembled skeletons because of the demands of forced labour and the lack of food.

Throughout that summer, Russian troops continued to advance further west and in the process liberated many other concentration camps across Poland and the Baltic States and captured the death camps of Belzec, Sobibor and Treblinka. The soldiers found little evidence of the mass murders that had been perpetrated at these camps. After an uprising at Sobibor, SS personnel demolished most of the camp following an order from Himmler to close it down on 19 October 1943 and few inmates survived more than a few months. In total, some 170,000 to 250,000 people were murdered at Sobibor, making it the fourth-deadliest Nazi camp after Auschwitz, Treblinka and Belzec. They demolished the gas chambers and most of the camp buildings, but left behind a number of barracks for future use by the German *Baudienst* ('building service' or 'construction service'). Once the destruction of the camp was complete and the apparatus used to murder the inmates was removed, the Jews that were left behind were shot. Trees were then planted on the site which was disguised as a farm.

Months later the Russians came across the site, but there was little evidence during that time of the mass murders inflicted there.

It was the same when Red Army soldiers liberated the Belzec death camp. The camp had operated from 17 March 1942 to the end of June 1943, and it was believed that between 430,000 and 500,000 Jews had been murdered there. When the camp closed down a clean-up commando of up to 500 prisoners remained in the camp, disinterring the bodies and burning them. Once the clean-up had been completed, the camp dismantled and all traces concealed in pits, the *Sonderkommando* ('work units') were transported to Sobibor and murdered on arrival.

Over the coming weeks and months Red Army units continued their remorseless advance westwards, coming across various camps including small satellite installations that were used for slave labour or civilian and PoW holding pens. On 17 January 1945 Russian soldiers captured the town of Chełmno. By then the Germans had long since destroyed evidence of the camp's murder installation. The camp had been specifically built for no other purpose than mass murder, operating from 8 December 1941 to 11 April 1943 in tandem with Operation REINHARD during its deadliest phase of the Holocaust. It is estimated that probably some 200,000 Jews from west-central Poland had been murdered at the camp. As news reached Himmler that the Russians were nearing some of the camps, especially those that still had incriminating evidence left behind, he ordered that a special detachment should undertake a clearing operation at Chełmno. In September 1944 the SS brought in a new Commando 1005 of Jewish prisoners from outside the Wartheland District to exhume and cremate remaining corpses and to remove evidence of the mass murder operations. A month later, the SS executed about half of the eighty-man detachment after most of the clearing operation was deemed complete. The gas vans were sent back to Berlin.

Following the liberation of Chełmno, ten days later Soviet troops would march along a road towards the town of Auschwitz and come across the largest mass murder factory of the Nazi regime.

In August 1944 the former commandant of Auschwitz, *SS-Obersturmbannführer* Rudolf Höss, had left southern Poland for Oranienburg and resumed his duties as Inspector of Concentration Camps. By this point in the war almost 6 million Jews had been murdered throughout the concentration camp system and millions more incarcerated in slave labour camps. It was estimated that the Nazis had established some 15,000 camps in the occupied countries during the war years. There were a number of smaller temporary camps constructed, often used to contain the local population before they were moved to larger camps for slave labour or to their deaths. The majority of these camps were destroyed by the Germans themselves, often only operating for a matter of weeks or months.

Rudolf Höss and his inspectorate were now concentrating on dismantling a number of camps and killing prisoners or moving them from one camp to another. By this time the military situation had changed dramatically. Although the camps mercilessly continued with the killings, the situation on both the Eastern and Western Fronts had deteriorated considerably for the Germans. Out in the East, German troops were fighting frantically to stem the Russian onslaught and by some incredible efforts they had managed to slow down their enemy. However, the whole German position in the East was now cracking, and any hope of repairing it was made almost impossible by crippling shortages of troops. To make matters worse, the Russians were now fighting on Polish soil east of Warsaw. On 6 September, as further battles in Poland intensified, Himmler suddenly ordered the liquidation of Auschwitz, including plans for the complete destruction of all four crematoria including Bunkers I and II. The order emphasized that all the personal effects from the warehouses as well as building materials and equipment were to be transported by motor vehicle and train back to the Reich. Half the 150,000 prisoners that were held captive in Auschwitz, most of them Poles and Russians, were to be moved to concentration camps in the West. Höss was informed that Buchenwald, Bergen-Belsen, Dachau, Flossenbürg, Gross-Rosen, Mauthausen, Natzweiler and Ravensbrück were to receive the Auschwitz prisoners.

By the end of 1944 approximately 500,000 prisoners were working in German factories, many of them from the vast pool of prisoners in the concentration camps. At Auschwitz and the surrounding sub-camps, those fit enough to be evacuated were ordered to be force-marched back to Germany and used as slave labour. Just two months earlier the *Reichsführer* had ordered the cessation of extermination operations across the Reich. At Birkenau the *Sonderkommando* had dismantled all the killing apparatus. The incineration ditches had also been cleared and levelled, and pits that had been filled with ash and the crushed bones of murdered prisoners were emptied and covered with fresh turf and other plants. Crematorium I in the main camp had been turned into an air-raid shelter and the chimney and holes in the ceiling through which Zyklon B had been thrown in were removed. All the furnaces of Crematoria I, II, III and IV were dismantled and the usable parts transported to other camps. On the night of 17 January some 58,000 prisoners were evacuated from Monowitz and the Auschwitz sub-camps, with about 20,000 coming from the Auschwitz-Birkenau camp alone. Very few were evacuated by train, with the majority of them being forced into the snow and marched in freezing night-time temperatures westward towards Germany. As they shuffled along the icy road, behind them the night sky was illuminated by flashes and the distant sounds of Russian gunfire rumbled across the horizon. Anyone including children that was unable to keep pace with the mass exodus was shot and their murdered corpses left at the roadside. Such scenes were utterly terrible.

Amid the chaotic evacuation order, the small groups of SS left behind at Auschwitz were given instructions for the demolition of the crematoria including Bunkers I and II.

After having blown up the remaining shells of Crematoria II and III in the early afternoon of 20 January, six days later they dynamited Crematorium V. As for Crematorium IV, this building had been demolished after it had been damaged by fire following a revolt in October 1944 by *Sonderkommando*. During the demolition of the crematoria special SS units murdered around 700 prisoners at Birkenau and nearby sub-camps. As news of the Red Army advanced along the main road from Krakow, the guards were ordered to destroy the last of the camp records, set fire to the Kanada stores (warehouse units), and liquidate the remaining prisoners in the camp. However, more concerned with saving their own lives than following orders the SS guards fled the camp, leaving the soldiers of the 1st Ukrainian Front to liberate Auschwitz and its sub-camps.

News of the events at Auschwitz had been closely observed by Höss, and its capture only reinforced his darkest fears of retribution if caught by the Russians. In fact, just days before its capture Höss had decided to drive to Poland personally to make sure that everything was destroyed as ordered, but due to advancing Russian forces he could only travel as far as the River Oder near Ratibor. Nevertheless, in spite of his growing concern about the advancing Red Army he helped direct the evacuation order of some of the Auschwitz prisoners west into the Sudetenland. According to Höss, he met officers from Auschwitz that had vehicles, and was determined to utilize whatever transport could be found to evacuate the prisoners westward. He even considered using the railway, but this was in a state of chaotic disorder.

During the frantic evacuation many of these railroad cars had been abandoned by the guards and left with the prisoners still inside, frozen to death in the sub-zero temperatures. On the roads conditions were just as unfavourable. With hardly any transport, thousands had been forced to march on foot with countless people dying in the arctic conditions. While some died of the cold and hunger, many were killed because they were too weak to keep up with the forced march.

Over the days and weeks that followed, the evacuations continued mercilessly. Throughout the evacuation there were scenes of utter confusion that were made worse by *Volksdeutsch* refugees trying to escape from the Red Army's advance.

On 27 January 1945, at 1500 hours the Soviet 322nd Rifle Division arrived at Auschwitz. In the surrounding area there had been some heavy fighting around Monowitz, Birkenau and the Auschwitz main camp. What greeted the soldiers was 'pure horror'. Many of these soldiers were battle-hardened men that had fought viciously through the Ukraine and into Poland and were used to seeing death. However, they were shocked by the appalling sight as they entered the camps. Red Army General Vasily Petrenko, commander of the 107th Infantry Division, said:

> I who saw people dying every day was shocked by the Nazis' indescribable hatred toward the inmates who had turned into living skeletons. I read about

the Nazis' treatment of Jews in various leaflets, but there was nothing about the Nazis' treatment of women, children and old men. It was in Auschwitz that I found out about the fate of the Jews.

Some 7,000 prisoners had been left behind, the majority of which were weak, malnourished and very sick. Most of the inmates were middle-aged adults or children less than 15 years of age. Soldiers found 600 corpses that had died in the barracks and stable huts. In the Kanada stores at Birkenau and at Auschwitz main camp they counted 370,000 men's suits, 837,000 articles of women's clothing and 7 tonnes of human hair. At the Monowitz camp, there were about 800 survivors. The camp was liberated by soldiers of the Soviet 60th Army, which was part of the 1st Ukrainian Front.

Photograph taken following the liberation of the Majdanek concentration camp, which was liberated by the Red Army on 22 July 1944.

Two photographs showing a view of the Majdanek concentration camp after its liberation. Initially the camp held a large number of Soviet prisoners and then around March 1942 it was refurbished as a killing centre.

The first of four photographs showing the double barbed-wire fences that enclosed Majdanek. It was the first major concentration camp liberated by Allied forces, and the dreadful evidence of mass murders found there by Russian soldiers was widely publicized.

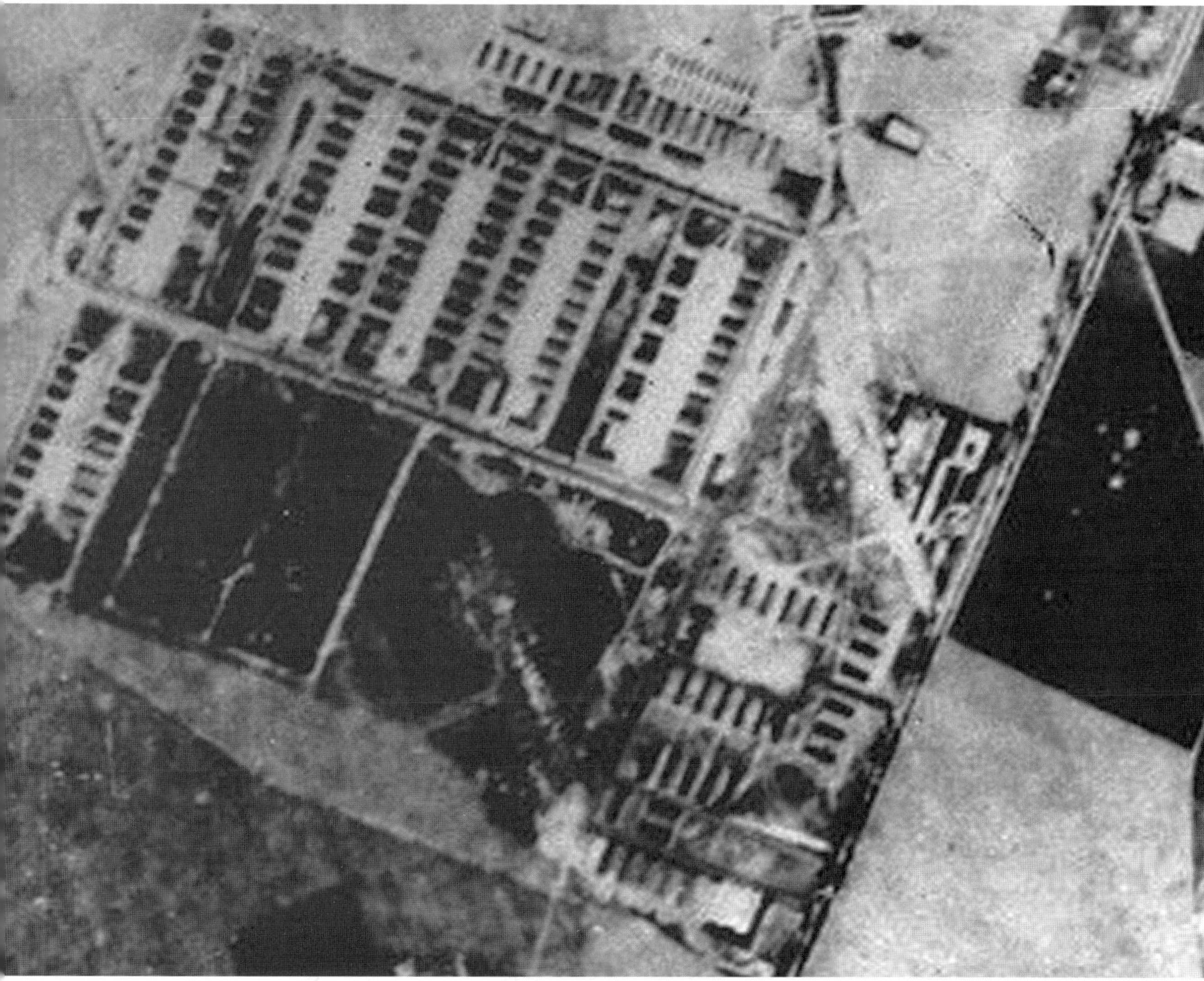

An aerial view of Majdanek. *(NARA)*

A guard post at the entrance to Field III in Majdanek.

Four photographs taken by Red Army soldiers following the liberation of Majdanek. The pictures detail the gas chambers and the rear and side of a gas chamber furnace. Note the second photograph showing the furnace that was used to create carbon monoxide for gassing inmates. The other two photographs show Soviet soldiers surveying the ovens and crematoria.

(**Above**) A photograph showing the crematoria at Majdanek. Initially Soviet troops did not understand what they had come across when they arrived at the camp. They had not been ordered to capture the installation. However, when they saw the high walls and the large gate, they thought it was sufficiently important to inspect. They then thought that the brick buildings, smokestacks and barracks were some kind of large factory or industrial plant. However, as the soldiers opened the doors to a gas chamber, an officer explained to them what they were about to see and how it operated. Not long afterwards, they came across a crematorium that was still warm.

(**Opposite, above**) A warehouse filled with containers of Zyklon B (poison gas pellets) at the Majdanek death camp. The Soviet war correspondent Konstantin Simonov was flown into Lublin to write about the camp. It was Simonov who was the first to describe a gas chamber. He also observed the canisters of Zyklon B and wrote about the enormous piles of shoes that were overflowing warehouses on the grounds of the camp: 'In one of the rooms of the camp offices, its floor literally carpeted with documents, were identification papers and passports belonging to the victims.' He went on to say that 'an immense number of Jews [were] brought to the camp to be exterminated from literally every country in Europe, from Poland to Holland.'

(**Opposite, below**) This is the site where the SS shot and burned the last forty-five of forty-eight prisoners at Chełmno when the camp was being evacuated. Russian soldiers captured the town of Chełmno on 17 January 1945. By then the Germans had already destroyed evidence of the camp's existence, leaving no prisoners behind.

ACHTUNG! TODESZONE!
UWAGA! STREFA SMIERCI!
СТОЙ! НЕПЕРЕСТУПАЙ
ГРОЗИТ СМЕРТЬЮ!
D.G.S. 24044
Gift
D.G.S. 24070
Gift

(**Above**) A Polish-Soviet Special Commission interrogates camp commandant *SS-Obersturmführer* Anthony Themes in Majdanek. He was eventually tried at the Majdanek trials and executed on 3 December 1944 along with five other war criminals near the gas chambers of the Majdanek crematorium.

(**Opposite**) Two photographs showing an aerial view of barracks at Auschwitz-Birkenau following the liberation of the camp by Red Army soldiers from the 322nd Rifle Division. The soldiers arrived at Auschwitz on 27 January 1945 at 1500 hours.

A view of the perimeter fence of the Auschwitz-Birkenau concentration camp after its liberation.

The electrified fence at Auschwitz-Birkenau. The sign reads 'Caution! High voltage. Danger to life.'

Russian soldiers converse with inmates inside Auschwitz-Birkenau. Some 7,000 prisoners had been left behind, most of whom were seriously ill due to the effects of their imprisonment.

Russian soldiers seen speaking to liberated prisoners at the Auschwitz main camp outside Block 19. The camp authorities designated Blocks 19, 20, 21 and 28 as the 'camp infirmary' for sick prisoners. Prisoners often referred to them as waiting rooms for the crematoria.

Three photographs taken in sequence showing prisoners liberated at the Auschwitz main camp gate with its infamous slogan inscribed *'Arbeit Macht Frei'* ('Work sets you free').

MACHT FRE

(**Opposite**) Two photographs taken in sequence showing children at the Auschwitz main camp following the liberation. During the camp's years of operation, many children in Auschwitz were subjected to medical experiments by the notorious Nazi physician Josef Mengele.

(**Above**) Child survivors of Auschwitz wearing adult-size prisoner jackets standing behind a barbed-wire fence.

(**Left**) Liberated inmates behind the barbed-wire fence at Auschwitz.

Two photographs taken in sequence showing former women prisoners on the wooden bunks that served as beds in the Auschwitz concentration camp.

Bales of hair from female prisoners, numbered for shipment to Germany, were found in the warehouses following the liberation of Auschwitz.

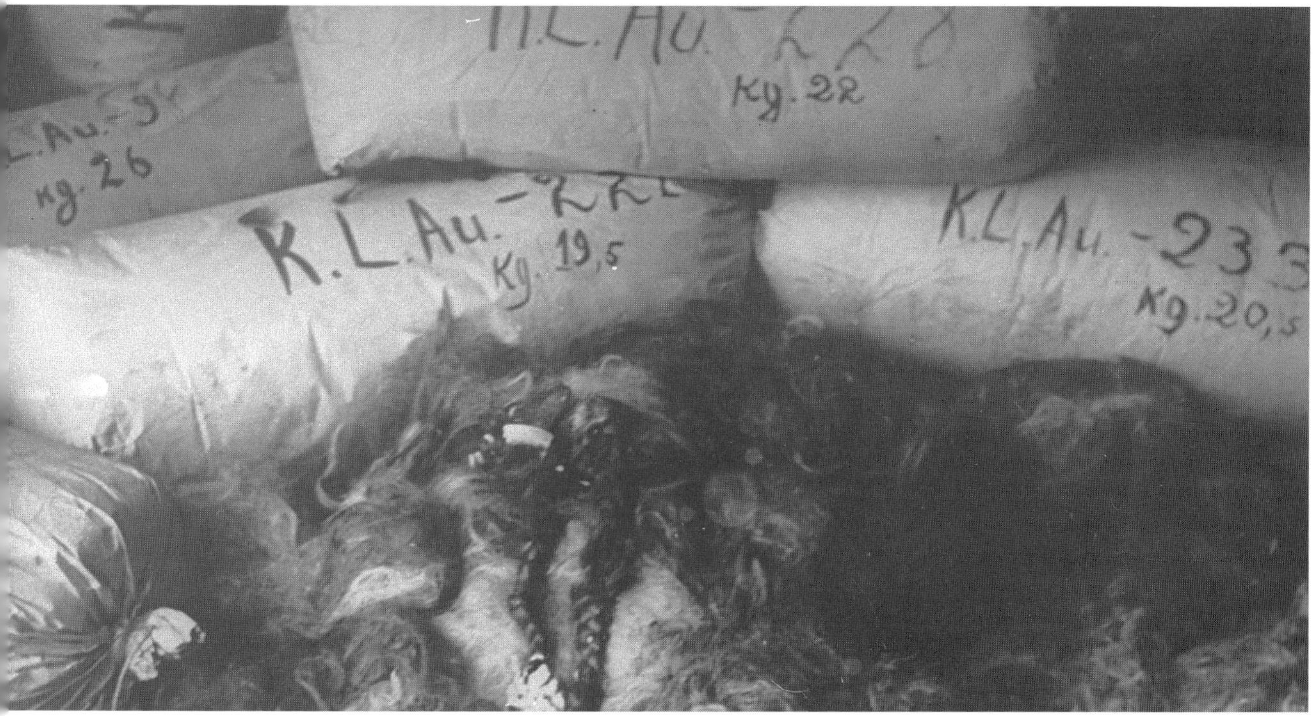

View of one of the warehouses in Auschwitz, which was overflowing with clothes confiscated from prisoners.

Soviet soldiers explore the remains of one of the four crematoria buildings at Auschwitz-Birkenau after the liberation.

Chapter Two

Liberation of German and Austrian Concentration Camps by US Forces

By early 1945, Allied forces in Europe were slowly advancing eastwards towards Germany. The failure of the German Ardennes Offensive in Belgium had exhausted their strategic reserves, leaving them ill-prepared to resist the final Allied campaigns in Europe. All available reserves the Germans could muster were thrown into the receding front lines in order to try to stall the Allied advance. By the third week of March 1945, American units were beginning to cross the Rhine. At the end of the month the British 8th Armoured Division was east of the Rhine and the encirclement of the Ruhr had begun in earnest. As these Allied successes gathered momentum, evacuation orders of some of the concentration camps in Germany were sent out to the various camp commandants.

In early April 1945, as US forces were advancing, the US 4th Armored Division led by Brigadier General Joseph F.H. Cutrona and the 89th Infantry Division entered Ohrdruf concentration camp, the first camp to be liberated by the US Army. The camp was built in November 1944 and became a sub-camp of Buchenwald. It had been one of the many 174 such sub-camps that had been erected during its operation. By late 1944, some 10,000 prisoners were housed there. Three months later the number had doubled to 20,000. The camp imprisoned mainly Jews, Poles, Russians, Hungarians and a mixture of French, Italians, Belgians, Czechs, Greeks, Yugoslavians and Germans. Conditions were terrible. As the SS monitored the advance of the Americans, an evacuation order was immediately sent out instructing that all inmates were to be marched out of the camp to Buchenwald on 1 April. During the march some 1,000 prisoners, malnourished, weak and sick, were shot by members of the *Hitlerjugend* and *Volkssturm* (national militia) and buried in a shallow grave. Later, in order to conceal the evidence of the mass murders, SS guards came back, reopened the grave and attempted to burn the corpses in the open air, using wooden frames as a cremation pyre in order to try to incinerate the bodies as quickly as possible. When

American soldiers arrived in the camp they discovered the piles of half-burned bodies partially incinerated on the smouldering pyre. The soldiers were faced with unthinkable conditions which made an indelible impact on all the men including General Dwight D. Eisenhower, General George S. Patton and General Omar Bradley, who all inspected the camp a few days later.

Over the next few days more sub-camps were liberated by the Americans including Langenstein. Nearby the Buchenwald commander had already hastily evacuated the camp between 6 and 11 April. In total some 28,000 prisoners were forced out of the main camp. The remaining 21,000 prisoners were left behind, deemed unfit for labour. In fact, as Americans occupied the surrounding areas, Gestapo headquarters at Weimar telephoned the Buchenwald camp administration to tell them that there had been an order to destroy the camp and kill all the remaining prisoners. Explosives would be used to conceal any evidence of the camp's existence. However, what the Gestapo did not know was that when they telephoned the camp administrators they had already fled. A prisoner answered the phone and informed headquarters that explosives would not be needed as the camp had already been blown up. This was obviously not true.

On 11 April, having secured the local area the 80th Infantry Division was ordered to take control of the Buchenwald concentration camp. Buchenwald was among the first large concentration camps liberated by the Americans. It was one of the first and the largest of the concentration camps within Germany's 1937 borders and was intended to hold just 8,000 prisoners, most of whom were political. The area was extended and included many sub-camps as the SS began to use forced labour for armaments production. Buchenwald was expanded and included up to 1,000 women by the end of 1944.

When US troops walked into the camp, there was much apprehension and horror about what they found. An American soldier from the 6th Armoured Division, Lieutenant William Cowling reported:

> Slowly, as we formed up, a ragged group of human beings started to creep out of and from between the buildings in front of us. As we watched these men, the number and the different types of buildings came to my attention. From them came these human beings, timidly, slowly, deliberately showing their hands, all in a sort of uniform, or bits and pieces of a uniform, made from horribly coarse cloth with stripes running vertically, the stripes alternating between a dull gray [*sic*] with a dark blue. Some of those human beings wore pants made of the material, some had shirt/jackets and some had hats. Some only had one piece of the uniform, others had two, many had all three parts. They came out of the buildings and just stood there, making me feel foolish with all of that firepower hanging on me. I certainly wouldn't be needing it with these folks.

He went on to say that they drove through a gate with the inscription *'Arbeit Macht Frei'* ('Work sets you free') to the other side of a building where they witnessed 'the bodies of human beings'. They were 'stacked like cord wood,' he said,

> All of them dead. All of them stripped. The inspection I made of the pile was not very close, but the corpses seemed to be all male. The bottom layer of the bodies had a north/south orientation, the next layer went east/west, and they continued alternating. The stack was about 5 feet high, maybe a little more; I could see over the top. They extended down the hill, only a slight hill, for 50 to 75 feet. Human bodies neatly stacked, naked, ready for disposal. The arms and legs were neatly arranged, but an occasional limb dangled oddly. The bodies we could see were all face up. There was an aisle, then another stack, and another aisle, and then more stacks. The Lord only knows how many there were.

On the same day that Buchenwald was liberated, Nordhausen-Dora was also freed by US troops. As the American forces advanced, the SS quickly evacuated most of the Mittelbau camps. In great haste and with significant cruelty, the prisoners were forced to march through the Harz Hills or were loaded onto a number of trains destined for Bergen-Belsen, Ravensbrück or Sachsenhausen.

Another camp liberated by American forces in April was Dachau, one of the first concentration camps built and the longest-running, opening on 22 March 1933. The installation was enlarged to encompass inmates for slave labour, and included Jewish prisoners, Romani and criminals from Germany and Austria including a variety of foreign nationals from across Europe. During its operation Dachau grew to include 123 sub-camps, all located in Germany and Austria. When news reached the commandant of Dachau in mid-April that US forces were advancing through Austria, he sent a message to Himmler requesting that the camp be handed over to the Americans. The *Reichsführer* forbade such a move and signed a correspondence outlining that 'no prisoners shall be allowed to fall into the hands of the enemy alive.' The camp was evacuated and 6,500 prisoners started a death march from Dachau south to Eurasburg and then eastwards towards Tegernsee. Those who survived the march would eventually fall into the hands of a US Army artillery battalion. More than 1,000 people died during the march. As for Dachau itself, on 28 April Victor Maurer, a representative of the Red Cross, negotiated an agreement to surrender the camp to the Americans. Hours later units of the 3rd Battalion, 157th Infantry Regiment, 45th Infantry Division commanded by Lieutenant Colonel Felix L. Sparks were ordered to secure the camp. The next day on 29 April the battalion entered the camp over a side wall. Simultaneously, the 222nd Infantry Regiment at the entrance of the camp and compound for the SS garrison accepted the formal surrender. More than 30,000 prisoners were liberated, consisting of Jews and political prisoners. In the surrounding area the sub-camps were liberated as well.

A week before the liberation of Dachau American troops liberated Flossenbürg concentration camp located in the Fichtel Mountains of Bavaria. The camp was operational from May 1938 and initially was built for slave labour for the production of granite. By 1943, the majority of prisoners were forced to manufacture Messerschmitt Bf109 fighter aircraft for the war effort. By mid-April Flossenbürg including its ninety-four sub-camps contained some 46,000 prisoners. Once again, as news reached the camp that the Americans were advancing, an evacuation order was sent out instructing Jewish inmates to be moved to the Theresienstadt Ghetto. Evacuation of non-Jewish prisoners began on 17 April following an order from Himmler instructing the camp commandant not to allow any prisoners to fall into enemy hands. Two days later the evacuation began with some 27,000 prisoners from the camp and sub-camps being moved to Dachau. Flossenbürg was liberated on 23 April by the US 90th Infantry Division. However, at many of the sub-camps the SS murdered sick Jewish prisoners before they fled, including killing prisoners on their death march.

The last camp liberated by the Americans was Mauthausen concentration camp built in upper Austria. The camp operated from August 1938 until its liberation on 5 May 1945. The camp was constructed for slave labour due to its location which included quarries and mines. During its operation Mauthausen together with its forty-nine sub-camps was used for munitions factories, arms factories and plants for assembling the new Messerschmitt Me262 jet fighter. By January 1945, some 85,000 prisoners were working in the camps. As the Red Army launched a series of heavy attacks against Hungary, the camp commandant feared Mauthausen might possibly be captured. Given the worsening military situation, he ordered remaining prisoners to quickly construct a line of granite anti-tank obstacles. However, many of the inmates were often too weak for heavy work and as a result were murdered by the SS. In early May as US forces approached, all work in the sub-camps was stopped and the SS guards were ordered to start evacuation of the prisoners and send them on a death march. In Mauthausen most of the camp personnel deserted, leaving the prisoners to their fate.

On 5 May a squad of US Army soldiers of the 41st Reconnaissance Squadron of the US 11th Armoured Division, Third US Army approached Mauthausen. When the troops entered the camp they found that around thirty guards who had decided to remain had been killed by the prisoners. By the next day all the remaining sub-camps, except for two located in the Loibl Pass, had been liberated by American soldiers.

(**Opposite, above**) A view of a section of the Ohrdruf concentration camp that includes a watchtower, barracks and barbed-wire fencing. This installation was a forced labour camp and a sub-camp of Buchenwald.

(**Opposite, below**) An American soldier drives past buildings set on fire by survivors after the SS evacuated the Ohrdruf concentration camp. By late 1944, around 10,000 prisoners were housed here, and through till March 1945 the total number sent here was around 20,000; mainly Russians, Poles, Hungarian Jews, some French, Czechs, Italians, Belgians, Greeks, Yugoslavians and Germans.

(**Above**) General Patton converses with General Omar Bradley during their tour of the newly liberated Ohrdruf concentration camp. It was liberated on 4 April 1945 by the 4th Armoured Division led by Brigadier General Joseph F.H. Cutrona and the 89th Infantry Division.

(**Opposite, above**) When the soldiers of the 4th Armoured Division entered the camp, they discovered piles of bodies, some covered with lime and others partially incinerated on pyres. In this photograph SS guards had burned some of the piles of bodies on a section of railroad track during the evacuation of the camp. Their charred remains are evident.

(**Opposite, below**) A photograph showing the charred remains of prisoners that were burned on a section of railroad track during the evacuation of the camp. General Dwight D. Eisenhower and a party of high-ranking US Army officers including General Omar Bradley, General George S. Patton and General Eddy were on an inspection tour of the camp.

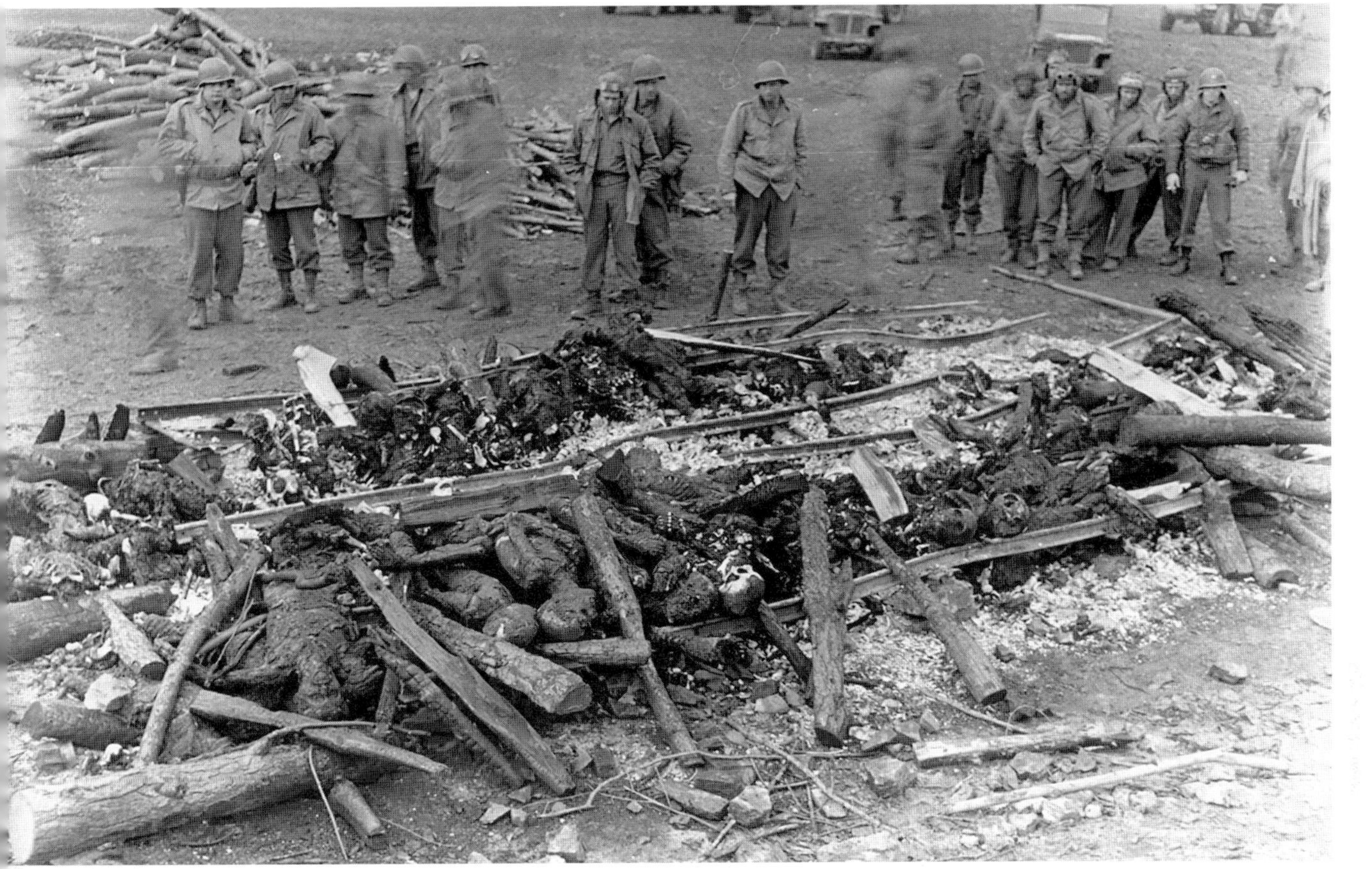

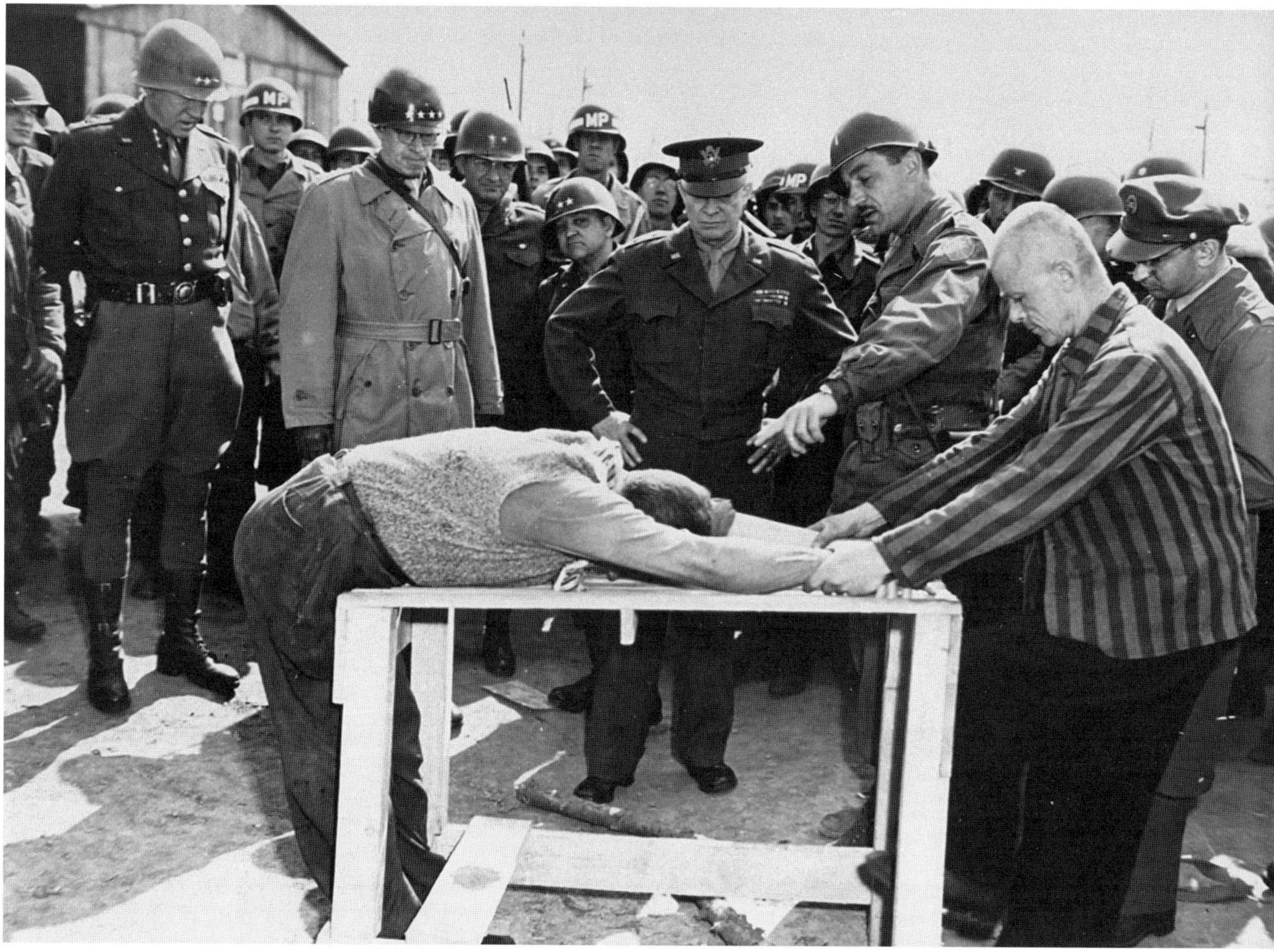
MP
MP
MP
MP

(**Opposite, above**) Survivors of the Ohrdruf concentration camp demonstrate to top-ranking American generals some torture methods used in the camp.

(**Opposite, below**) The bodies of prisoners executed by the SS prior to the evacuation are laid out in a wooded area near the Ohrdruf concentration camp.

(**Above**) General Dwight D. Eisenhower and General Troy Middleton tour the newly liberated Ohrdruf concentration camp.

(**Above**) The Flossenbürg concentration camp after its liberation. On 14 April 1945, *SS-Reichsführer* Heinrich Himmler ordered all the camps to be evacuated. He instructed that 'Not a single prisoner must fall alive into enemy hands.'

(**Opposite, above**) A section of the barbed-wire fence and barracks in the Flossenbürg concentration camp.

(**Opposite, below**) The interior of a barracks in the Flossenbürg concentration camp that was intended to house 1,500 prisoners. The camp was liberated by US soldiers who arrived on 23 April 1945 where they found 2,500 surviving inmates.

Visiting radio commentators on an official tour of the war front wait at the entrance to the newly liberated Buchenwald concentration camp.

A French survivor shows the crematorium in Flossenbürg to a photographer. Due to increased mortality from the harsh conditions at the camp, the SS had ordered the construction of an on-site crematorium, which was completed in May 1940.

Escorted by American soldiers, a transport of child survivors of Buchenwald files out of the main gate of the camp. A detachment of troops of the US 9th Armoured Infantry Battalion from the 6th Armoured Division, part of the US Third Army, arrived at Buchenwald on 11 April 1945 at 1515 hours. (The clock at the main gate was later altered and set to the time of the liberation.)

An emaciated survivor drinking from a metal bowl in front of a barracks in Buchenwald.

Joseph Schleifstein, a 4-year-old survivor of Buchenwald, sits on the running board of a UNRRA truck soon after the liberation of the camp.

Jewish men, women and children at a roll-call in Buchenwald for departure to Switzerland shortly after the liberation of the camp.

(**Opposite, above**) Survivors lie in multi-tiered bunks in a barracks in the newly liberated Buchenwald concentration camp.

(**Opposite, below**) A large heap of ashes and bones shovelled out of the crematoria ovens in Buchenwald concentration camp.

(**Above**) A delegation from the International Red Cross views the gallows during a tour of Buchenwald after the liberation.

(**Above**) Large quantities of items including cutlery and other objects from Buchenwald were found in crates hidden in a nearby cave along with other boxes of confiscated belongings.

(**Opposite, above**) An American captain with survivors in the Buchenwald concentration camp.

(**Opposite, below**) A Russian survivor liberated by the 3rd Armoured Division of the US First Army identifies a former camp guard who brutally beat prisoners. In fact after General George S. Patton had toured the camp to see for himself the horror of what the Nazis had done at Buchenwald, he ordered the mayor of Weimar to bring 1,000 citizens to the camp; these were to be predominantly men of military age from the middle and upper classes. The Germans had to walk a roughly 16-mile round trip under armed American guard and were shown the crematorium and other evidence of Nazi atrocities.

(**Above**) Liberated Jewish children wave goodbye as they depart by train from the Buchenwald concentration camp in June 1945.

(**Opposite, above**) Two survivors lie among corpses on the straw-covered floor of the barracks called the Boelcke Kaserne Nordhausen. US troops of the 3rd Armoured Division, 104th Infantry Division and 9th Infantry Division reached Nordhausen on 11 April 1945. There were also around 1,300 dead prisoners at the barracks.

(**Opposite, below**) Two emaciated survivors sit outside on the stoop of a barracks in the newly liberated Nordhausen concentration camp.

(**Above**) A Polish survivor shows US soldier John L. Lyndon the crematorium ovens used to burn corpses in Dora-Mittelbau.

(**Opposite, above**) German civilians from the town of Nordhausen carry the bodies of prisoners from the Nordhausen concentration camp to mass graves.

(**Opposite, below**) A second photograph in the sequence shows German civilians from the town of Nordhausen digging mass graves for the victims of the camp.

(**Above**) The building that housed police officials at Dachau, shown after liberation. On 28 April 1945 units of the 3rd Battalion, 157th Infantry Regiment, 45th Infantry Division commanded by Lieutenant Colonel Felix L. Sparks were ordered to secure the camp. The next day Sparks led part of his battalion and entered the camp over a side wall. What they found was a total horror.

(**Opposite, above**) Survivors and US troops at the entrance to the Dachau concentration camp.

(**Opposite, below**) A view of the electrified barbed-wire fence, the moat and the watch tower in Dachau.

B
E3

(**Opposite, above**) An aerial view of the Dachau concentration camp.

(**Opposite, below**) A view of the Kaufering IV concentration camp, a sub-camp of Dachau, taken on the day of liberation.

(**Above**) German civilians from the town of Hurlach move corpses found in Kaufering IV to mass graves for burial.

(**Opposite, above**) Corpses lay in a pile beside the charred ruins of barracks in the Kaufering IV concentration camp.

(**Opposite, below**) A US Signal Corps cameraman, Joseph Wright of the 103rd Infantry Division, films evidence of Nazi atrocities in Kaufering IV. The original caption reads: 'The Landsberg Atrocity: A Signal Corps cameraman records the horror of Landsberg prison. In the smoking remnants of their burned prison hut lie charred and emaciated bodies of Jewish prisoners burned alive by Nazi prison guards who locked them in their wooden huts and set them afire before retreating before the Seventh Army.'

(**Above**) American soldiers in Kaufering IV look at the bodies of prisoners killed by the SS prior to the arrival of US forces.

(**Above**) German civilians from the town of Hurlach are forced to carry corpses to mass graves for burial.

(**Opposite, above**) Troops with the medical detachment of Combat Command A, 12th Armoured Division, XXI Corps, US Seventh Army examine the bodies of prisoners killed by the SS just prior to the evacuation of the camp. The original caption reads: 'Landsberg Atrocity: The emaciated bodies of victims of German cruelty at Landsberg prison. Before retreating in the face of the Seventh Army attack, the Jewish prisoners were locked in their huts and told they would be shot if they came out. Then the buildings were set on fire. Some burned to death in their huts, others found strength to break down the doors and crawl out to die in the streets. Most prisoners were naked. Some had remnants of clothing on their charred bodies. Here medics examine corpses in front of the ruins of a charred hut.'

(**Opposite, below**) German civilians in Hurlach push a wagon laden with corpses to a mass grave for burial.

(**Above**) Survivors lay in multi-tiered bunks in the infirmary in the Dachau concentration camp soon after its liberation.

(**Opposite, above**) A watch tower and section of the electric fence in Dachau.

(**Opposite, below**) Survivors look out of the barbed-wire-covered windows of barracks in the newly liberated Dachau concentration camp.

(**Above**) Suspected members of the *Hitlerjugend* ('Hitler Youth') are forced by American troops of the US Seventh Army to view the Dachau death train.

(**Opposite, above**) SS personnel in Dachau surrender to troops of the US 45th Infantry Division.

(**Opposite, below**) American soldiers execute SS camp guards who had been lined up against a wall during the liberation of the Dachau concentration camp. The number of SS members executed is disputed as some were killed in combat, some while attempting to surrender and others after their surrender was accepted. In 1989, Brigadier General Felix L. Sparks, the colonel in command of a battalion that was present, stated: 'The total number of German guards killed at Dachau during that day most certainly does not exceed fifty, with thirty probably being a more accurate figure. The regimental records of the 157th Field Artillery Regiment for that date indicate that over a thousand German prisoners were brought to the regimental collecting point. Since my task force was leading the regimental attack, almost all the prisoners were taken by the task force, including several hundred from Dachau.'

208765

B
167
206304

(**Opposite**) The bodies of SS guards, who were shot by American troops, lay on the edge of the moat at the base of a guard tower in Dachau. An Inspector General report resulting from a US Army investigation conducted between 3 and 8 May 1945 titled 'American Army Investigation of Alleged Mistreatment of German Guards at Dachau' found that twenty-one plus 'a number' of presumed SS men were killed, with others being wounded after their surrender had been accepted.

(**Above**) An American soldier stands beside the bodies of SS personnel shot by US troops during the liberation of Dachau.

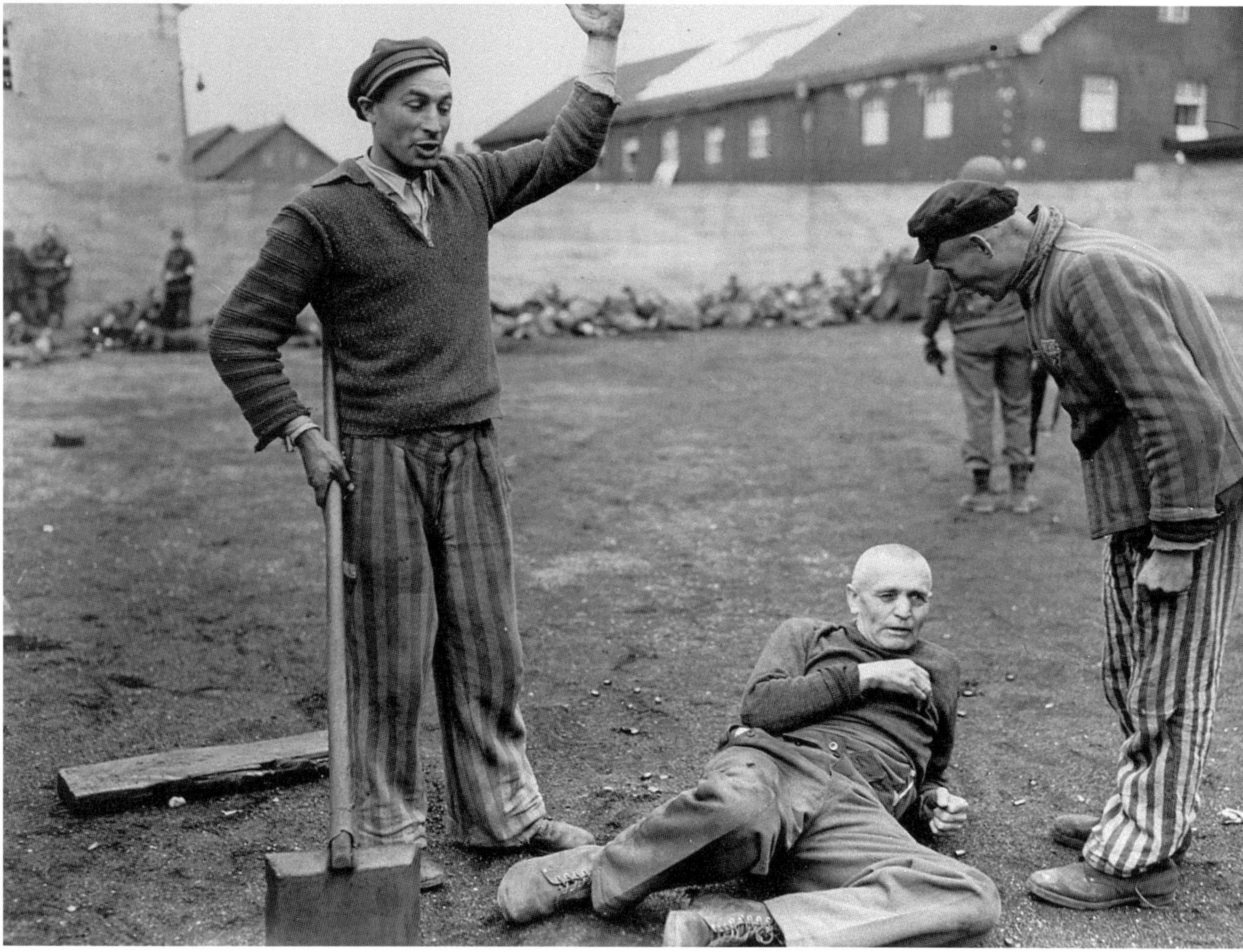

(**Above**) Survivors in Dachau shout and physically attack an SS guard captured by US troops, while in the background American soldiers summarily execute other camp guards.

(**Right**) A survivor in Dachau, photographed on the day of liberation.

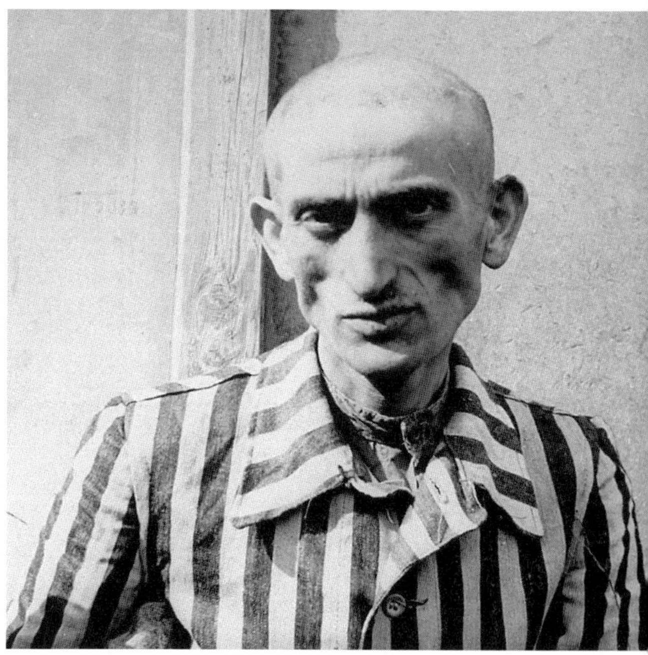

(**Opposite, above**) A prisoner lends assistance to two US troops as they fish the body of an SS guard out of the moat surrounding the Dachau concentration camp.

(**Opposite, below**) Survivors cheer the arrival of the American liberators of Dachau.

A soldier from the US Seventh Army examines the door to a gas chamber in the Dachau concentration camp.

The new crematorium in Dachau, which was completed in May 1944.

Survivors fight for cigarettes thrown to them by American troops after the liberation of the Dachau concentration camp.

(**Above**) Two American soldiers examine disinfected prisoner uniforms in Dachau.

(**Opposite, above**) Survivors stand behind the barbed-wire fence in Dachau. Immediately following the liberation of the camp, authorities worked continuously to try to improve the terrible conditions. An epidemic of black typhus had already swept through the camp and by 3 May 2,000 cases had already been reported.

(**Opposite, below**) Prisoners' barracks in the Dachau concentration camp.

B

Survivors in the Ampfing concentration camp are deloused after their liberation by men of the 14th Armoured Division, US Third Army.

Two photographs taken in sequence showing young and old survivors in Dachau cheering as US troops enter the liberated camp.

(**Above**) The crematoria at Dachau. During the twelve years of its operation at the camp, it was recorded that some 206,206 prisoners passed through the gates of Dachau and some 31,951 died of disease and mistreatment. The crematoria were constructed to dispose of the dead.

(**Opposite, above**) Survivors gather to salute the Allies and remember comrades who died in Dachau.

(**Opposite, below**) Emaciated survivors in the shower barracks after the liberation of Dachau.

THE POLES SALUTE
LIBERATO

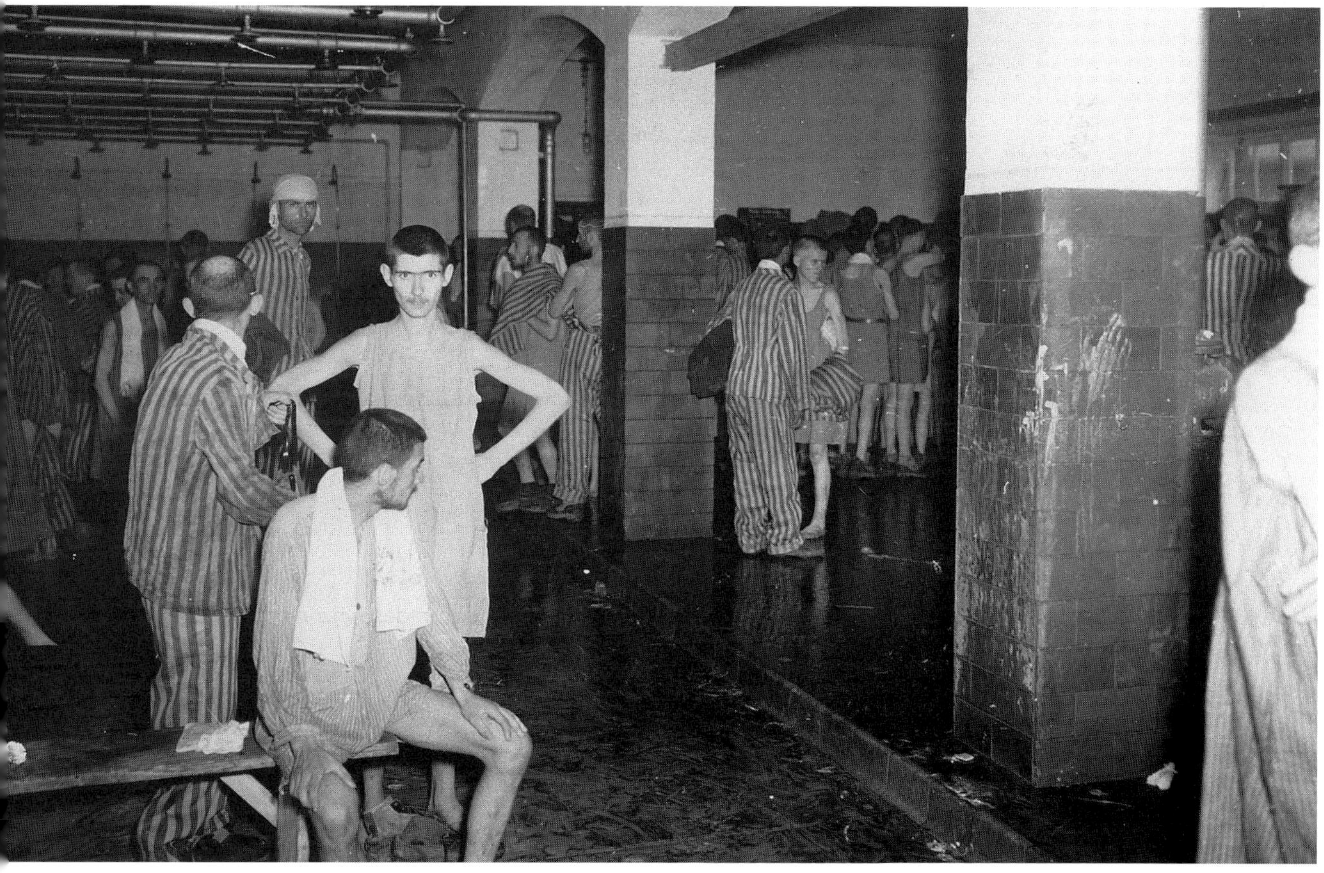

Two photographs, the first of which shows a view of the construction of the Gusen I concentration camp, and second is following its liberation. Gusen was a sub-camp of Mauthausen. In order to expand armaments production, the camp was re-designated Gusen I and additional camps, Gusen II and Gusen III, were built. Prisoners were forced to construct vast underground factories. Staff Sergeant Albert J. Kosiek, in charge of a platoon in the 41st Cavalry Squadron, was ordered to investigate a suspected enemy strongpoint near Mauthausen. Units arrived in the Gusen sub-camps on 5 May 1945 and liberated it.

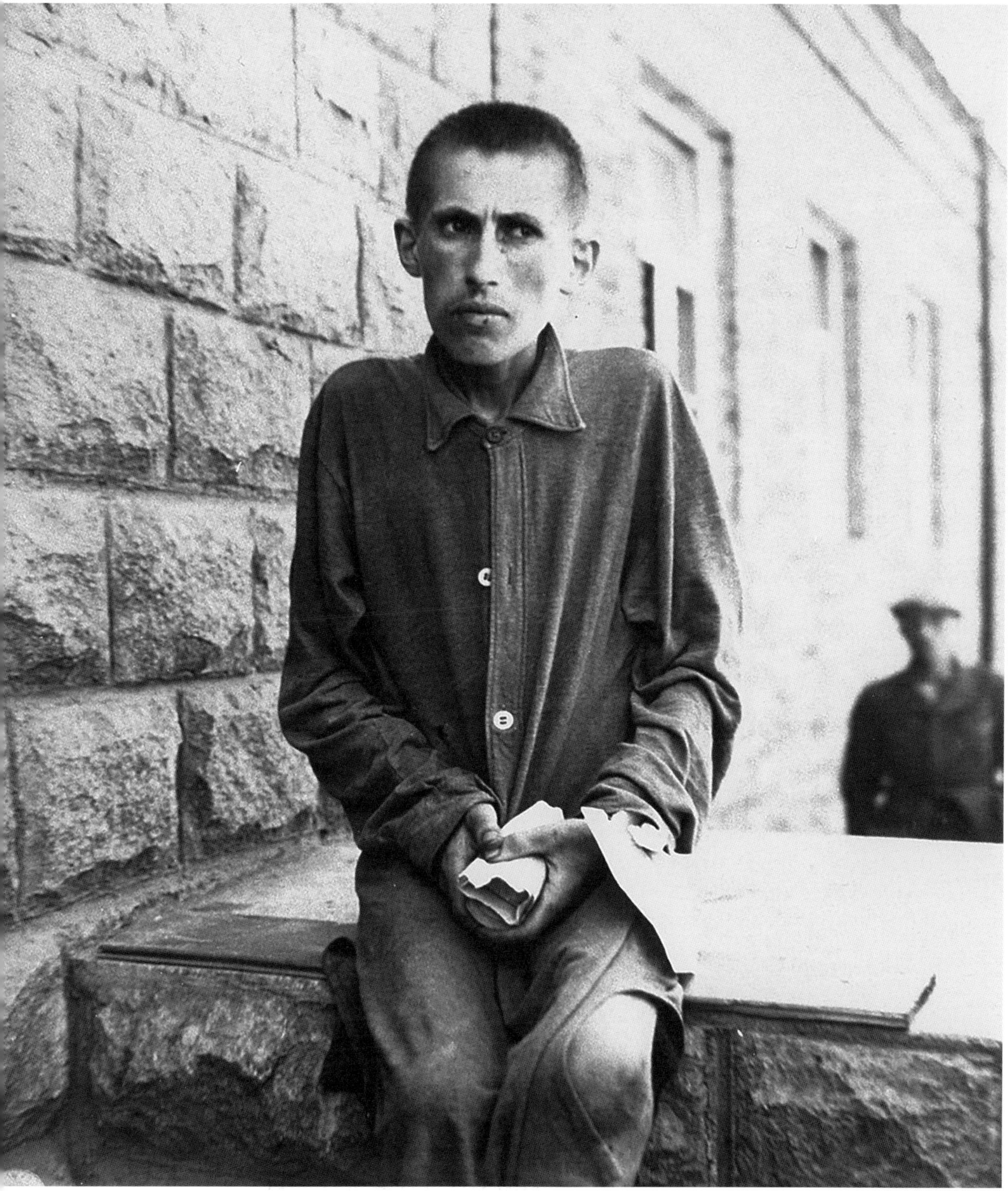

A close-up portrait of a survivor in Gusen shortly after the liberation of the camp.

(**Above**) Two female survivors sit outside in the newly liberated Gusen concentration camp.

(**Opposite, above**) Corpses in Gusen prior to their removal and burial by Austrian civilians.

(**Opposite, below**) Austrian civilians load corpses onto a cart that will transport the bodies to a mass grave at Gusen camp.

(**Above**) Crematorium furnaces in the Gusen concentration camp after liberation.

(**Opposite, above**) The 11th Armoured Division of the US Third Army views the corpse of a camp guard killed by survivors after its liberation.

(**Opposite, below**) Prisoners at the Ebensee concentration camp pose outside for the US Army Signal Corps. The Ebensee camp was a sub-camp of Mauthausen, which was built for armaments storage near the town of Ebensee, Austria in 1943. On 4 May 1945 the commandant of the camp informed prisoners that they had been sold to the Americans and that they should seek shelter in the camp's tunnels for protection. However, the inmates refused and remained in the barracks, fearing they would be killed. During the early hours of 5 May the SS guards fled the camp and left behind elderly Germans guarding the camp. The prisoners awoke to find that the SS had deserted Ebensee and only elderly Germans armed with rifles were left on guard. In reprisal for the cruelty inflicted on the inmates, the prisoners killed fifty-two camp functionaries who had collaborated with the SS to create the camp's hierarchy. US troops of the 80th Infantry Division arrived at the camp on 6 May and Ebensee was liberated.

Emaciated prisoners who had been starved receive sugar cubes provided by American soldiers in the infirmary barracks for non-Jewish prisoners in the Ebensee concentration camp.

Seven emaciated survivors stand naked behind the barbed-wire enclosure of the hospital compound in Ebensee.

A group of emaciated survivors prepare a meal on an open fire in the newly liberated Ebensee concentration camp.

Emaciated survivors sit on bunks in one of the infirmary barracks in the Ebensee concentration camp.

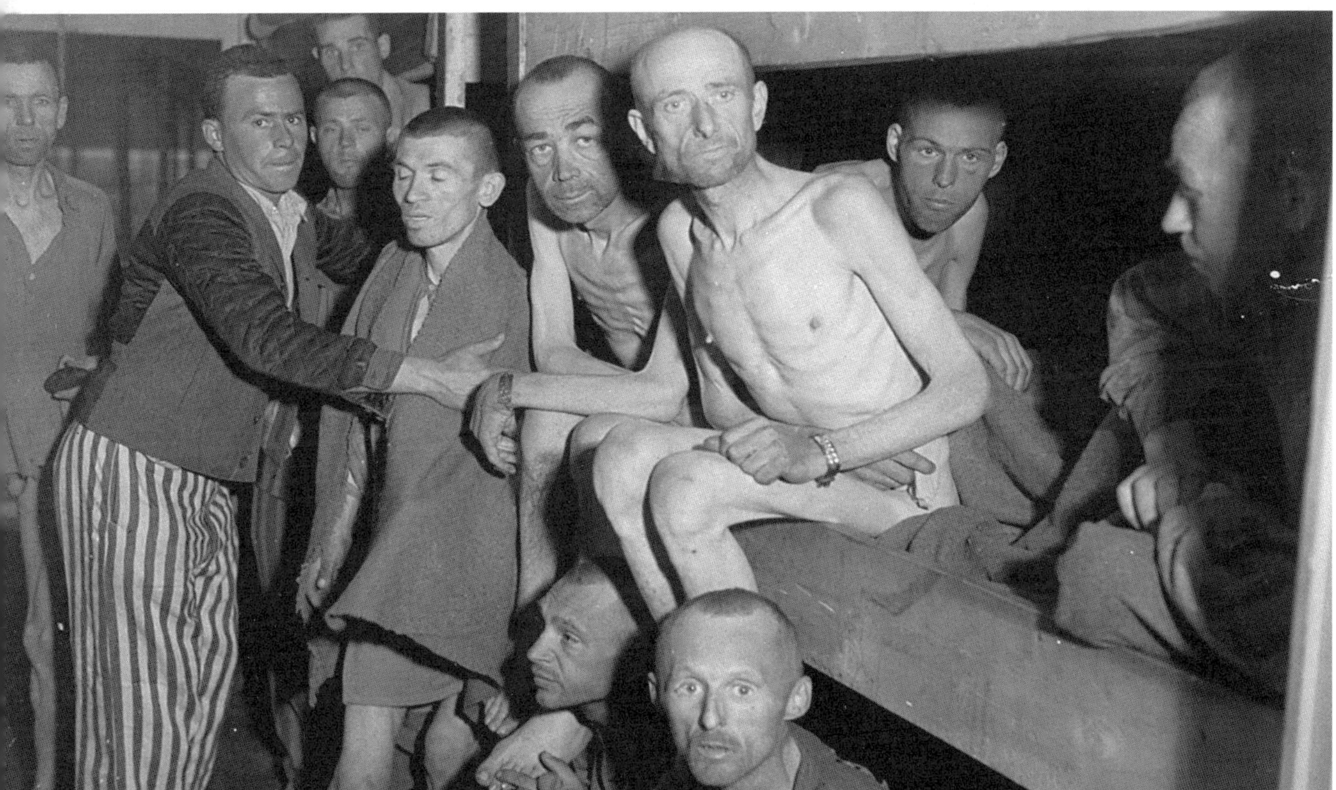

(**Above**) Survivors of the Ebensee concentration camp who were liberated by US Third Army troops march out of the camp beneath the sign 'We Welcome Our Liberators.'

(**Opposite, above**) Cheering survivors greet American troops as the first Allied tanks enter the Mauthausen concentration camp. On 5 May 1945 the US Army reached Gusen and Mauthausen. Some prisoners were in such weakened condition that many still died during the days and weeks after liberation.

(**Opposite, below**) Troops from an armoured division of the US Ninth Army survey one of the electric fences at Mauthausen.

(**Opposite, above**) The entrance to the SS compound at Mauthausen in 1942.

(**Opposite, below**) Spanish survivors take down the Nazi eagle that hangs above the entrance to the SS compound in Mauthausen on the day of liberation.

(**Above**) Mauthausen survivors cheer the soldiers of the 11th Armoured Division of the US Third Army one day after their actual liberation.

(**Above**) Half-starved prisoners inside a barracks after liberation glare at the camera. The bodies of dead prisoners have been piled up in the open area on the ground to the right.

(**Opposite, above**) Survivors in the quarantine camp section of Mauthausen after liberation.

(**Opposite, below**) A view of the Russian camp at Mauthausen. Many thousands of Russian PoWs were sent to the concentration camps and worked to death. At Mauthausen Russian inmates were used as slave labour for both the main camp and the sub-camps.

(**Above**) German civilians from Schwarzenfeld dig graves for the reburial of 140 Hungarian, Russian and Polish Jews exhumed from a mass grave near the town. They are watched by US soldiers.

(**Opposite, above**) Survivors walk along the main street of the Mauthausen concentration camp.

(**Opposite, below**) The bodies of two Dutch Jews who committed suicide by touching the high-tension fence in Mauthausen.

(**Opposite, above**) In the women's camp at Mauthausen survivors stand around the entrance to a barracks.

(**Opposite, below**) A view of 180 corpses piled outside a barracks in the Russian camp section of Mauthausen after liberation.

(**Above**) The bodies of prisoners shot by SS guards in Gunskirchen concentration camp prior to the liberation of the installation by American soldiers. These photos were taken by US troops. The SS guards had fled, leaving many corpses littering the camp. Some 15,000 prisoners were still in the place.

(**Opposite, above**) Prisoners can be seen here carrying a comrade who had escaped from the Wöbbelin concentration camp a few days before its liberation entering through the camp. Troops of the 82nd Airborne Division, US Ninth Army carried out its liberation.

(**Opposite, below**) Sick survivors are evacuated from the Wöbbelin concentration camp to an American field hospital where they will receive medical attention.

(**Above**) A survivor, thinking that US soldiers had forgotten to evacuate him from Wöbbelin concentration camp, breaks into tears in the compound and pleads to be removed.

(**Opposite, above**) Soldiers of the US 82nd Airborne Division look on as Germans exhume corpses from a mass grave at the Wöbbelin camp.

(**Opposite, below**) Survivors wait for evacuation from the Wöbbelin concentration camp to an American field hospital, where they will receive medical attention.

(**Above**) Survivors get water at one of the community pumps in the newly liberated Wöbbelin camp.

American soldiers patrol the perimeter of the newly liberated Wöbbelin camp.

Chapter Three

Liberation of German Concentration Camps by French, British and Canadian Forces

Following the success of the Allies in northern Europe in the summer of 1944 American, British, Canadian and French forces spearheaded through France, Belgium and Holland. One of the first concentration camps that the Allied forces came across in advancing through Holland was located in Vught near the town of 's-Hertogenbosch. The installation was known as the Herzogenbusch concentration camp. This camp operated between January 1943 and October 1944 and the inmates comprised mainly Jews, gypsies and political prisoners. On 26 October 1944, Scottish forces of the 7th Black Watch liberated the camp following heavy fighting with a rearguard of SS personnel left to defend the almost evacuated facility. Some 500 to 600 prisoners were liberated from the camp. Their lives were truly saved as they had been due for execution that afternoon. Many, however, had not been so fortunate and soldiers found some 500 dead inmates piled up near the gates, having been executed on the very morning of the day the camp was liberated.

Elsewhere Allied forces pushed across Europe. Along the borders of Germany located in the Vosges Mountains in the Gau Baden-Alsace was another camp discovered by the Allies: Natzweiler-Struthof. The camp operated between May 1941 and September 1944 and was the only concentration camp built by the Germans in the territory of pre-war France. It was estimated that some 50,000 prisoners were held at the camp during its operation. It was a labour and transit camp. However, as the Allies approached the camp was evacuated, leaving behind only a handful of SS guards when the French First Army under the command of the US Sixth Army liberated the camp on 23 November 1944.

As the Allies pushed further into Germany units began coming across more camps in their zone of operation, finally revealing how extensive the murderous activities of the Nazi regime had been. Littered across northern and southern Germany were various camps that ranged considerably in size. Some appeared to be like factories, while others were no more than small transit camps for temporarily holding prisoners before they were sent to other camps either to work or to die. One of the largest transit camps the British and Canadian forces came across in Lower Saxony was a place called Bergen-Belsen. In 1940 the installation was initially a prisoner-of-war camp, but by 1943 it had become part of the concentration camp system. At first it was bizarrely an exchange camp for Jewish hostages held with the intention of exchanging them for German PoWs held overseas. However, as the war progressed the camp was extended and more Jews were transported to Belsen. At its peak the camp totalled 120,000 inmates comprising Jews, Poles, Soviets, Dutch, Czechs, Germans and Austrians. During its operation some 70,000 died of starvation, illness, neglect, torture and murder. In fact, conditions were so bad that between 1943 and the end of 1944 some 3,000 people died. From January to mid-April 1945 that figure increased to around 35,000. This number also included the two sub-camps as well. Around 2,000 female prisoners were forced to work there. Those too weak to work were transported back to Belsen where they often died. Conditions were made worse as the Allies advanced. As more camps were being evacuated, the inmates were forced to go on death marches to Belsen, overcrowding the camp. Conditions by April were appalling, disease was rife and starvation was particularly common, in some instances leading to cases of cannibalism.

In mid-April as the Allies advanced on Belsen the Wehrmacht negotiated a truce and exclusion zone around the camp to prevent the spread of typhus. Due to the disease, Himmler decided to have the camp handed over to the enemy without any resistance. The *Reichsführer* was conscious of the dead, and ordered SS guards and prisoners to start burying the corpses in a pathetic attempt to conceal some of the horror. On 12 April Wehrmacht representatives met with the British, D Squadron of the Inns of Court Regiment at Winsen, and later drew up an agreement designating a 19-square-mile exclusion zone around the camp. The agreement also allowed the majority of the SS guards to leave. Only a small number of SS men and women including the notorious camp commandant *SS-Hauptsturmführer* Josef Kramer were ordered to stay at the camp. However, due to heavy fighting near Belsen the British 11th Armoured Division was unable to enter the camp until 15 April. American soldiers attached to the British unit also entered the camp and were shocked by what they saw: some 60,000 prisoners, the majority of which were half-starved and seriously ill, while another 13,000 corpses lay around the camp unburied. There were so many people in the camp that the soldiers were overwhelmed. Hungarian soldiers that were guarding the perimeter and exclusion zone were brought into the camp to assist. Kramer was quickly arrested. Under his command both the female and male guards had continued to uphold their mission to mistreat and kill the inmates. Despite news of the advancing Allies approaching the camp, the majority of the female guards did not attempt to prepare themselves for the inevitable post-war retribution. Even as enemy gunfire grew louder with each passing day, most of the women, unlike their male counterparts, never tried to gain favour with the inmates by treating them better, even when it was clear that the camp would be captured. With British forces advancing into the area, the female guards remained at their post. Walking around the camp, the soldiers were neither physically nor psychologically prepared for what they encountered when they arrived at the gates of the camp that day, being numbed and nauseated by what they saw, smelled and heard. Yet, even beyond this ugly spectacle, the liberation of the camp witnessed some strange moments. As the troops approached the main gate in a motorized column, SS personnel, as if preparing for a formal reception, were drawn up in their field grey uniforms. The SS guards appeared cheerful. Josef Kramer, for instance, seemed unusually outgoing, friendly and pleasant to the soldiers. However, behind them were thousands of the unburied dead in addition to the mass graves already containing another 40,000 corpses. At that time as many as 500 a day were perishing from the long-term effects of starvation as well as disease. When Kramer was questioned by the British he frankly and calmly spoke of the starving masses as if he were referring to cattle. He appeared more concerned that the British would use their loudspeakers, fearing it might cause the inmates to stampede. Then as the British moved further into the camp, the sound of periodic gunfire could be heard. SS guards were firing on inmates surging towards the kitchen in the hope of finding something to eat. One of the female guards, Irma Grese, the notorious 'beautiful beast', attacked a British general as he was attempting to enter some huts, but she was immediately restrained.

When the British came upon the women's compound, the troops were confronted by a formation of well-fed overweight female guards who were said to be just casually standing around chatting and smoking cigarettes while awaiting their arrest. All the women wore white brassards on their lower left tunic sleeves with a black cloth strip bearing the silver-threaded SS *Aufseherin* stamp. One soldier recalled that many of the women had contorted, ugly facial expressions and all wore either hob-nailed jackboots or military issue dress shoes with black socks.

Once the SS women were arrested, they joined the men on burial details. All of them had the gruesome task of dragging corpses to the pits. The soldiers noticed that the majority of the women reacted differently to this ghastly work than the men. While some of the men ran away from the ordeal and one committed suicide, none of the women attempted to avoid it.

Another camp that received many inmates was Neuengamme. This site had some ninety-six sub-camps in the Bergedorf district of Hamburg. The camp became the largest in north-west Germany, with more than 100,000 prisoners coming through Neuengamme and its sub-camps. It was established in December 1938 and by 1940 a crematorium was constructed in the camp. In the same year, the civilian corporations Messap and Jastram opened armament plants on the camp site and used the prisoners for slave labour. Over the course of four years the camp expanded and by the end of 1944, the total number of prisoners grew to some 49,000 with 12,000 in Neuengamme and 37,000 in the sub-camps, including almost 10,000 women in the various sub-camps. However, by March 1945 with the Allies advancing the sub-camps were evacuated on death marches to Belsen and Osnabrück. On 19 April an order instructed the main camp to be emptied and some 9,000 prisoners transported by ship for Norway in terrible conditions. On 2 May, the SS and the last of the prisoners left the Neuengamme concentration camp. Three days later the first British soldiers arrived and saw that the camp had been emptied. Lieutenant S. Charlton of the 53rd Reconnaissance Regiment who arrived in Neuengamme reported that his units had come across a number of camps by then, and he had been bracing himself for the worst. He found the site completely empty, with a civilian policeman guarding the entrance. He wrote: 'The camp had machine-gun posts and lookout towers.' He wasn't sure whether the wiring was electrical, but it 'looked as if it could have been'. As he was inspecting the barracks, 'two persons appeared'. These former prisoners offered to guide him through the camp and explained the purpose of the different buildings. 'To anybody who did not know about it,' Charlton said of one of these buildings, 'it appeared to be a butcher's shop or a dairy.' It was a 'medical experimental station'. The place appeared to have been thoroughly cleaned, and he only found 'rubber gloves and what [he] took to be a preserved human heart in a bottle.'

While British troops were advancing on the Belsen and Neuengamme sub-camps, on 12 April Canadian troops reached the Westerbork transit camp where they were welcomed with cheers. Some 900 prisoners remained in the camp. The Germans had quickly fled the advancing Allied army the day before. The camp had been opened by the Dutch authorities during the summer of 1939 in order to receive the Jewish refugees coming from Germany. By July 1942 German authorities had taken control of the camp and it became officially a transit camp to hold Jews that were being sent to Auschwitz. Between 1942 and 1945, 107,000 Jews were deported to the East from the Netherlands, mostly via Westerbork.

During April other transit and sub-camps were liberated. In almost every camp Allied soldiers encountered appalling scenes. As soon as they arrived, the liberating forces, often assisted by the Red Cross, tried to help survivors by organizing medical care and food. There were also efforts to try to document what had happened at the camp and report on their findings.

(**Opposite, above**) A sign warning of the electrified high-tension wire fence enclosing the transit camp. In October 1944, the British Second Army launched Operation PHEASANT in the Netherlands and came across this camp.

(**Opposite, below**) A photograph taken following the liberation of the Vught concentration camp. It shows a view of the barbed-wire fence, drainage ditch and watch towers. On 26 October 1944, Scottish troops of the 7th Black Watch liberated the camp during fierce fighting in what was known as Operation PHEASANT. Many of the SS personnel had evacuated the installation, leaving behind just a small contingent of SS guards.

Hochspannung
Lebensgefahr

(**Opposite, above**) This photograph is a closer view of the barbed-wire fence, with the drainage ditch and a watch tower in the background.

(**Opposite, below**) The entrance to the Natzweiler-Struthof concentration camp, which is being guarded by two members of the French Resistance.

(**Above**) A sign on the road to the Natzweiler-Struthof concentration camp warning that the camp is in the area and that those who approach it will be shot without warning. It was the French First Army under the command of the US Sixth Army that liberated the camp on 23 November 1944.

(**Above**) A young member of the French Resistance examines boots, shoes and wooden clogs piled up near a furnace in the crematorium of the Natzweiler-Struthof concentration camp.

(**Opposite**) Two photographs showing a section of the Bergen-Belsen concentration camp following its liberation. The camp was incorporated into the system in June 1943. In March 1944, part of the camp was re-designated as an *Erholungslager* ('recuperation camp') where other concentration camp inmates too sick to work were brought to supposedly recover. However, many of them died of disease, starvation, exhaustion and lack of medical attention.

13

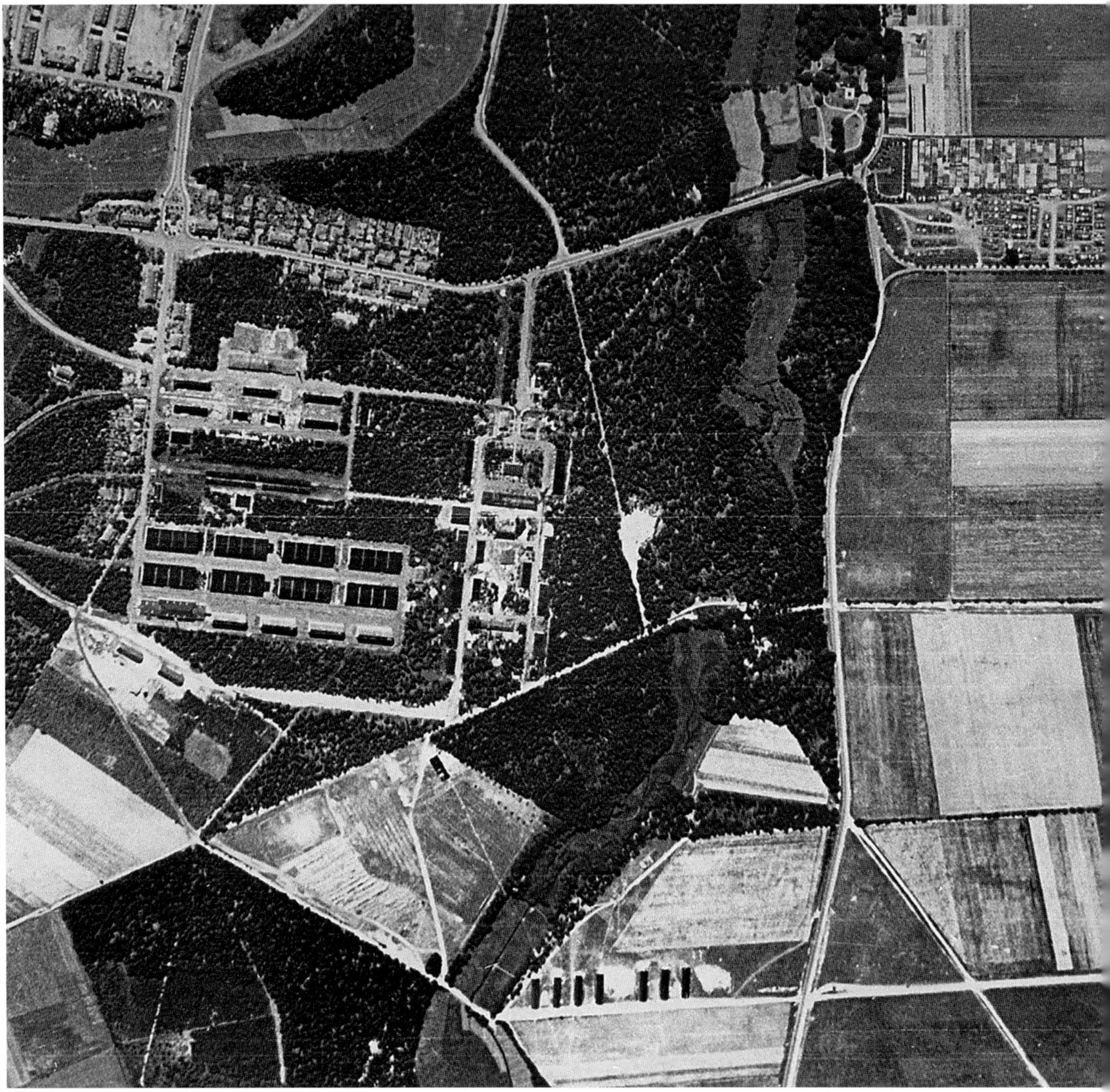

(**Above**) An aerial reconnaissance photograph of the military camp 1.5 miles from the Bergen-Belsen concentration camp area.

(**Opposite, above**) The commandant's office building in Bergen-Belsen. The notorious camp commandant *SS-Hauptsturmführer* Josef Kramer, dubbed 'the beast of Belsen', worked from here. He was responsible for the deaths of thousands of inmates at the camp, which was liberated on 15 April 1945 by the British 11th Armoured Division.

(**Opposite, below**) Corpses lying among survivors in Bergen-Belsen following its liberation.

(**Above**) The main road through Bergen-Belsen.

(**Right**) A photograph of one of the many emaciated female survivors found in Bergen-Belsen.

(**Opposite**) Two images taken in sequence showing some of the barracks inside the camp. As soon as the British entered, the soldiers immediately started to provide the survivors with emergency medical care, clothing and food.

(**Opposite, above**) Survivors sit among corpses that littered a section of Bergen-Belsen.

(**Opposite, below**) Survivors in Bergen-Belsen tend to chores after their liberation.

(**Above**) Liberated inmates peel potatoes while behind them lay the corpses of prisoners who had died before the liberation of the camp.

(**Opposite, above**) What appears to be Hungarian guards dusting survivors in Bergen-Belsen with DDT powder to help prevent the spread of typhus. Initially lacking sufficient manpower, the British allowed the Hungarians to remain in charge of the camp, including guard duties and assisting with the prisoners' needs and requirements.

(**Opposite, below**) The crematorium oven at Bergen-Belsen where prisoners were burned in their thousands.

(**Above**) The first of four photographs showing survivors inside their barracks in Bergen-Belsen after liberation.

(**Below**) A Hungarian sentry guarding the perimeter at Bergen-Belsen concentration camp on 28 April 1945. Due to the lack of guards, the Hungarians were used to help the British. These soldiers were no longer killing the inmates alongside their SS counterparts. In fact, during the liberation SS and Hungarian guards had actually shot and killed some of the starving prisoners who were trying to get their hands on food supplies from the storehouses. The British forced the former SS camp personnel to help bury the thousands of dead bodies in mass graves.

Evacuating female political prisoners from Bergen-Belsen.

Chapter Four

Liberation of German Concentration Camps by Soviet and Polish Forces

On the Eastern Front Russian forces were advancing at speed and arriving at the River Oder in preparation for their attack on the Reich capital of Berlin. As units continued their remorseless advance through Germany they came across numerous concentration camps. On 22 April Russian soldiers of the 1st Belorussian Front and Polish troops of the 2nd Infantry Division advancing through Oranienburg came across what was known as Sachsenhausen concentration camp. The camp had opened in July 1936 and held political prisoners and Russian PoWs. Many of the camp inmates were Jehovah's Witnesses, homosexuals, Freemasons and Poles. The place was primarily a slave labour camp with some forty-four sub-camps. Sachsenhausen itself was fitted with a gas chamber and a medical experiment area.

In December 1944, with the war situation deteriorating on the Eastern Front, the camp had already started the process of clearing some of the prisoners. All of the sick inmates were ordered on the instructions of Himmler to be executed or transferred to the death camps. Approximately 2,000 of them were removed. Two months later in February 1945, some 1,300 prisoners were killed during the evacuation of the Lieberose forced labour camp. As the Russians advanced through Germany during the spring, the commandant of Sachsenhausen was ordered to begin the evacuation of the camp. On 21 April the camp's SS staff ordered some 33,000 prisoners on a forced march north-west. Many hundreds died on the march due to exhaustion and those who collapsed were shot by the SS. The march ended near Raben Steinfeld in early May after the area was liberated by both Russian and American forces. At Sachsenhausen only 3,400 inmates were liberated by the Russians and Poles.

Following the liberation of Sachsenhausen, just over a week later Soviet forces came across another camp: Ravensbrück in northern Germany some 56 miles north of Berlin. It became operational in May 1939 and exclusively held women prisoners.

The majority of those held at the camp were political prisoners and the remainder were Jews. Ravensbrück comprised a main camp plus thirty-one sub-camps. In the spring of 1941, a small men's camp adjacent to the main site was established by the SS to use the inmates for work detail, with the SS authorities making use of them in building and managing the gas chamber for the camp in 1944. During its operation several thousand inmates were murdered by gassing. By early January 1945, it was estimated that some 45,000 female prisoners and more than 5,000 male prisoners remained at Ravensbrück. As the Russians advanced, the SS leadership ordered the clearance of prisoners from the surrounding sub-camps and sending them directly to the main camp gas chamber. The SS were determined to try to conceal their murderous activities by evacuating all inmates from the camp, and those sick and unable to march were to be gassed or shot. Some 24,000 prisoners comprising physically capable women were escorted in file out of the camp on a death march in the direction of northern Mecklenburg. Some 2,500 ethnic Germans were released and 500 women handed over to officials of the Swedish and Danish Red Cross. When the Russian soldiers entered the camp on 30 April, the SS had not had time to murder those left behind that were physically sick. Some 3,500 starved and sick inmates were liberated. Those that had been forced on the death march and had survived were liberated by a Russian scout unit. Angry about what the soldiers had witnessed in the camp, the Russians forced the local townspeople to help clean the camp and bury those who had died.

(**Below**) The Sachsenhausen concentration camp showing a view of the prisoners' barracks with Nazi slogans painted on the front. On 22 April 1945, the camp's remaining 3,400 inmates were liberated by the Russian 1st Belorussian Front and the Polish 2nd Infantry Division.

(**Opposite, above**) On one of the fences at Sachsenhausen a sign reads 'No entry or you will be shot.' Just a day before the camp's liberation the SS staff ordered some 33,000 inmates on a death march north-west, which ended near Raben Steinfeld in early May 1945.

(**Opposite, below**) A Russian photograph showing some of the many thousands of garments in huge piles outside one of the storage barracks when the camp was liberated.

Verbotene
Zone
Eintritt verboten.
Es wird geschossen!

(**Above**) Two photographs showing the Ravensbrück concentration camp that was built exclusively for women. On 30 April 1945, fewer than 3,500 malnourished and sick prisoners were discovered alive at the camp when it was liberated by the Red Army.

(**Opposite, above**) Women prisoners at Ravensbrück can be seen here behind one of the fences during the camp's liberation. Just before the Russians arrived, the SS forced some 24,000 inmates to go on a death march.

(**Opposite, below**) Surviving female prisoners gathered when the Red Cross arrived at Ravensbrück in April 1945. The white painted crosses indicated that they were not civilians but prisoners of the camp.

(**Opposite, above**) A photograph of the service building in May 1945 following the liberation of Ravensbrück.

(**Opposite, below**) Russian soldiers discover Ravensbrück's crematoria. According to estimated figures, during the camp's operations some 130,000 female prisoners passed through the camp. Around 50,000 of them died from disease, starvation and overwork, while around 2,200 were murdered in the gas chambers.

(**Above**) By the appearance of these prisoners liberated from Ravensbrück they do not appear to have been at the camp too long. They had also been spared the death march.

Polish women from Ravensbrück converse with a Russian doctor.

What appears to be a Russian nurse assisting and caring for two liberated women at Ravensbrück.

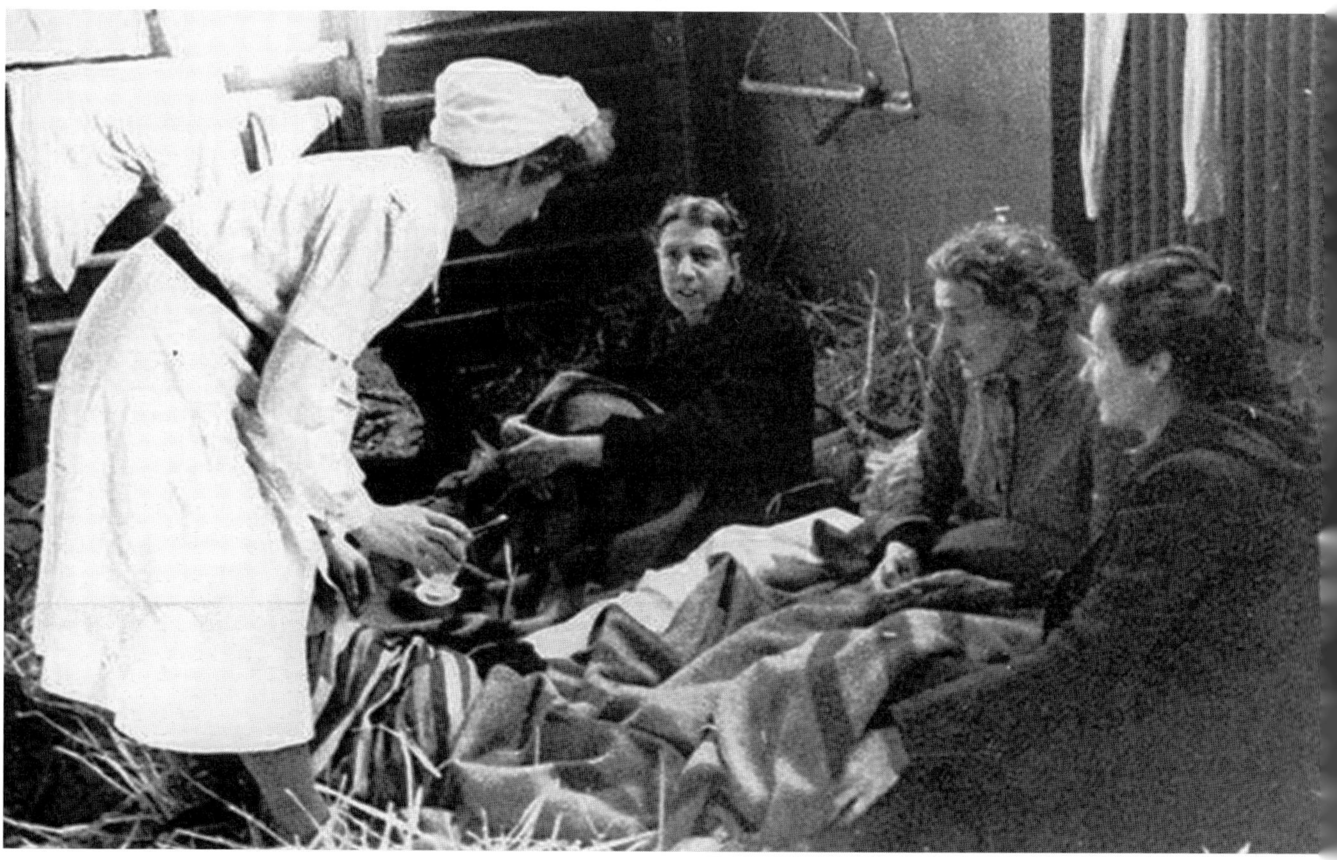

A photograph taken by a Soviet photographer showing a group of liberated women from Ravensbrück.

A view of the Stutthof concentration camp after its liberation by the Red Army on 9 May 1945.

Appendix I

List of Concentration Camps and Sub-Camps

The majority of these camps were either dismantled or destroyed by the German authorities, often within weeks of their operation.

Germany

Bergen-Belsen (probably 2 sub-camps, location is not known)

Börgermoor (no sub-camp known)

Buchenwald (174 sub-camps)
Buchenwald/Dora-Mittelbau
Abterode
Adorf
Allendorf
Altenburg
Annaburg
Arnstadt
Arolsen
Artern
Ascherleben
Baalberg
Bad Berja
Bad Godesberg
Bad Handersheim
Bad Salzungen
Ballenstadt
Baubrigade I-X
Bensberg
Berga/Elster
Berlstedt
Bernburg
Billroda
Birkhan-Motzlich
Bischofferode
Blankenburg
Blankenheim
Bleicherode
Bochum I
Bochum II
Bodtenberg
Böhlen
Braunschweig
Buttelstedt
Clus
Coblence: 'rebstock'
Colditz (Hasag)
Cologne I
Cologne II
Cologne III
Crawinkel
Dernau
Dessau I
Dessau II
Dornburg
Dortmund
Duderstadt
Düsseldorf I
Düsseldorf II
Düsseldorf III
Eisenach
Ellrich
Elsnig
Eschenhausen
Escherhausen
Essen I
Essen II
Flossenbürg
Freiheit-Osterode
Gandersheim
Gelsenkirchen
Giessen
Gleina
Goslar
Göttingen
Grasleben
Grosswerther
Günzerode
Hadmersleben
Halberstadt
Halberstadt-Zwieberge
Hardehausen
Harzungen
Hasserode
Herzberg/Elster
Hessich-Lichtenau
Hinzert
Hohlstedt
Holzen
Ilfeld
Ilsenburg
Jena
Kassel
Kelbra

Klein bischofferode
Klein bodungen
Klein niedergerba
Kleinnoshersleben
Köln fordwerke
Köln hansestadt
Köln westwagen
Kranichfeld
Langensalsa
Langenstein
Lauenberg 'Laura'
Lehensten 'Laura'
Leimbach
Leipzig (Hasag)
Leipzig Lindenthal
Leipzig Markkleeberg
Leipzig Schönauer
Leopoldshall
Lippstadt
Lohausen
Lützkendorf
Magdeburg I
Magdeburg II
Markkleeberg
Merseburg
Meuselwitz
Muhlhausen 'Martha'
Neustadt
Niederorshel
Niedersachswerfen
Nordhausen I
Nordhausen II
Nordhausen III
Nuxei
Oberndorf
Ohrdruf
Oschersleben 'Ago'
Osterhagen
Osterode
Penig (Gehrt)
Plomnitz
Quedlinburg I
Quedlinburg II
Raguhn
Rehmsdorf 'Willy'
Römhild
Rossla
Rothenburg
Rottleberode
Saalfeld-Örtelsbruch
Salza-Thuringe
Sangerhausen
Schlieben (Hasag)
Schönau
Schönbeck (Hasag)
Schwalbe V
Schwerte
Sennelager
Sollstedt
Sömmerda
Sonneberg
Stassfurt
Stutzpunkt Sauerland 1
Suhl
Tannenwald
Tanndora
Taucha (Hasag)
Thekla (Erla-Werke)
Tonndorf
Torgau
Trautenstein
Troglitz (Brabag)
Unna
Walkenried-Wolfleben
Wansleben
Wansleben 'Biber II'
Wansleben 'Wilhelm'
Weimar
Weimar-Fischtenhain
Werferlingen
Wernigerode
Westeregeln
Wewelsburg
Wickerode
Wieda
Witten-Annen
Wöbbelin
Wolfen
Wuppertal
Zeitz 'Willy'
Zella Mehlis
Zorbig

Dachau (123 sub-camps)
Aibing
Allach
Allach/Karsfeld/Moosach
Allach-Rothwaige
Allersdorf-Liebhof
Ampersmoching
Asbach-Baumenheim
Aufkrich-Kaufbeuren
Augsburg
Augsburg-Haunstetten
Augsburg-Pfersee
Augustenfeld-Pollnhof
Bad Ischl
Bad Ischl Saint Wolfgang
Bad Tolz
Bad Bayernsoien
Baubrigade XIII
Bayrishezell
Bichl
Birgsau-Oberstdorf
Blainach
Brunigsau
Burgau
Burghausen
Burgkirchen
Donauworth
Durach-Kottern
Eching
Ellwagen
Emmerting-Gendorf
Eschelbach
Feistenau
Feldafing
Fischbachau
Fischen
Fischhorn/Bruck
Freising
Friedolfing
Friedrischaffen
Fulpmes
Fussen-Plansee

Gablingen
Garmisch-Partenkirchen
Germering-Neuaubing
Gmund
Grimolsried-Mitteneuf-Nach
Halfing
Hallein
Hausham-Vordereckard
Heidenhaim
Heppenhaim
Horgau-Pfersee
Hurlach
Ingoldstadt
Innsbruck
Itter
Karlsfeld
Kaufbeuren
Kaufering
Kaufering Erpfting
Kempten-Kotern
Königssee
Krucklhalm
Landsberg
Landshut-Bayern
Lauingen
Lechfeld
Liebhof
Lind
Lochau
Lochhausen
Lohof
Markt Schwabben
Mettenheim
Mittel-Neufnach
Moosach
Moschendorf-Hof
Muldorf
Muldorf Ampfing-Waldlager V and VI
München
München Friedman
München Riem
München Schwabing
München Sendling
Neuburg Donau
Neufahrn
Neustift
Nuremberg
Oberdorf
Oberföhring
Obertaufkirchen
Ottobrunn
Ötztal
Passau
Puchheim
Radolfzell
Riederloh
Rohrdorf-Thansau
Rosenheim
Rothschwaige-Augustenfeld
Salzburg
Salzweg
Sandhoffen
Saulgau
Schlachters-Sigmarszell
Schleissheim
Schwabbeg
Schwabmuünchen
Seehausen-Uffing
Spitzingsee
St. Gilden/Wolgansee
St. Lambrecht
Steinhöring
Stephanskirchen
Strobl
Sudelfeld
Traustein
Trotsberg
Trutskirch-Tutzing
Turkenfald
Turkheim
Überlingen
Ulm
Unterschleissheim
Utting
Valepp
Vulpmes
Weidach
Weilheim
Weissensee
Wicking
Wolfratshausen
Wolfratshausen Gelting
Wurach-Wolhof
Zangberg

Altenhammer
Annaberg
Ansbach
Aue (Sachsen)
Bayreuth
Beneschau
Bozicany
Brüx
Chemnitz
Dresden
Eisenberg
Erbendorf
Falkenau
Flöha
Forrenbach
Freiberg
Ganacker
Giebelstadt
Grafenreuth
Graslitz
Gröditz
Gundelsdorf
Hainichen
Happurg
Heidenau
Helmbrechts
Hersbruck
Hertine
Hof
Hohenstein-Ernstthal
Holleischen
Holyson
Hradischko
Hubmersberg-Hohenstadt
Janowitz
Jezeri
Johanngeorgenstadt
Jungfern-Breschan
Kaaden-Kadan
Kamenicky-Senow
Kirchham
Knellendorf

Königstein
Krondorf
Leitmeritz
Lengenfeld
Lobositz
Mehltheuer
Meissen
Mittweida
Moickethal-Zatschke
Moschendorf
Mülsen-St. Michel
Münchberg
Neu Rohlau
Nossen
Nuremberg
Obertraubling
Oederan
Olbramowitz
Pilsen
Plattling
Plauen
Pocking
Porschdorf
Poschetzau
Pottenstein
Praha
Rabstein
Rathen
Rathmanndorf
Regensburg
Reuth
Rochlitz
Saal/Donau
Schlackenwerth
Schönheide
Seifhennersdorf
Siegmar-Schönau
St. Georgenthal
St. Ötzen
Stein-Schönau
Stulln
Theresienstadt
Venusberg
Wilischthal
Witten-Annen
Wolkenburg
Würzburg
Zatschke
Zschachwitz
Zschopau
Zwickau
Zwodau

Ahlem-Hannover
Altegarde-Elbe
Altgarga
Aumund
Aurich-Engerhafe
Bad Sassendorf
Barkhausen
Barskamp
Baubrigade I, II, V and XI
Beendorf-Helmstedt
Bergstedt
Blumenthal
Boizenburg
Braunschweig
Bremen-Farbe
Bremen-Osterort-Reisport
Bremen-Schützenhof
Bremen-Vegesack-Aumund
Bremen-Weser
Brink-Hannover
Brunswick-Busing
Dalum
Dreutte
Engerhafe
Fallersleben-Laagberg
Farge
Fidelstedt
Finkenwerder
Fuhlsbüttel
Geilenberg
Glassau-bei-Sarau
Goslar
Gross-Fullen
Gross-Hesepe
Hamburg
Hausberge-Porta
Helmstadt
Hidelsheim
Horneburg
Howachts-Lütjenburg
Kaltenkirch-Heinkaten
Kiel
Laasberg
Ladelund
Langenhagen-Hannover
Langenhorn-Hamburg
Lengerich
Lerbeck
Limmer-Hannover
Linden
Lübberstadt
Ludwigslust
Lüjtenburg
Meppen
Minden
Misburg-Hannover
Mölln
Neesen
Neugraben
Neuhof
Neuland-Bremen
Neunkirchen
Neustadt
Nutzen
Ohldorf
Osnabrück
Osterort
Poppenbüttel-Sasen
Porta-Westfalica
Salzgitter
Salzwedel
Sandbostel
Sasel
Schandelah
Schützenhof-Bremen
Schwessing-Husum
Sollstadt
Spaldingstrasse
Steinwerder
Stöcken-Hannover
Stuklenwert
Tiefstak
Uelzen
Veerssen
Vegesack-Aumun-Bremen

Veleen
Verden-Aller
Wandsbeck
Watenstedt-Drütte-Salzgitter
Wedel
Wilhemsburg-Hamburg
Wilhemshaven
Wittenberge
Wolfsburg
Wöbbelin-Ludwigslust

Dieburg (no sub-camp known)
Esterwegen (1 sub-camp)
Flossenbürg (94 sub-camps)
Gundelsheim (no sub-camp known)
Neuengamme (96 sub-camps)
Papenburg (no sub-camp known)

Ravensbrück (31 sub-camps)
Abteroda
Ansbach
Barth/Ostee
Belzig
Berlin-Oberschöneweide
Berlin-Schönefeld
Borkheide
Bruckentin
Comthurey
Dabelow
Eberswalde
Feldberg
Fürstenberg
Hennigsdorf
Herzebrück
Hohenlychen
Karlshagen
Klützow-Stargard
Köningsberg-Neumark
Malchow
Neubrandenburg
Neustadt/Glene
Peenemünde
Prenzlau
Rechlin
Retzow
Rostock-Marienhe
Schwarzenforst
Stargard
Steinhöring
Uckermark
Velten

Sachsenhausen (44 sub-camps)
Babelsberg
Bad Saarow
Baubrigade I, II, III, IV, V, VI, VII, VIII, IX, X, XI and XII
Beerfelde
Berga
Berlin
Falkensee
Helensee (Demag)
Hennigsdorf (AEG)
Köpenick
Lichtenrade
Lichterfelde
Reinickendorf (Argus)
Siemens Stadt
Tegel
Wilmersdorf

Biesenthal
Bornicke
Brandenburg/Havel
Dammsmühle-Schönwalde
Debno-Neudamm
Döberitz
Drogen-Niedorf
Falkenhagen-Fürstenwalde
Falkensee
Friesoythe/Cloppenburg
Genshagen
Glau-Trebbin
Gross-Rosen
Heinkel
Hohenlychen
Karlsruhe
Kleinmachnow
Klinker
Kolpin
Königs Wusterhausen
Küstrin
Lieberose
Lubben
Muggelheim
Neubrandenburg (Hamburg)
Neustrelitz
Niederhagen
Oranienburg
Politz
Prettin
Rathenow
Ravensbrück (until 1939)
Riga
Senftenberg/Schwarzweide
Storkow
Stuttgart
Treuenbrietzen
Werde
Wewelsburg
Wittenberg (Arado)

Sachsenburg (no sub-camp known)

Austria

Mauthausen (49 sub-camps)
Aflenz
Redl-Zipf (code-name Schlier)
Amstetten (2 camps: male and female)
Bachmanning
Bretstein
Diepoldsau
Ebelsberg
Ebensee
Eisenerz
Enns
Floridsdorf
Grein

Grossraming
Gunskirchen
Gusen I, II, III
Hinterbrühl
Hirtenberg
Klagenfurt
Kleinmünchen
Leibnitz
Lenzing
LindLinz I, II, III
Loibl – Pass Nord
Loibl – Pass Süd (ex-Yugoslavia)
Melk
Mittersill
Passau I – Waldwerke
Passau II
Peggau
St. Agyd
St. Lambrecht
St. Valentin
Steyr
Ternberg
Vöcklabrück/Wagrain
Wels
Wien Afa-Werke
Wien Saurer-Werke
Wien-Schwechat
Wien Schönbrunn
Wiener Neudorf
Wiener Neustadt

Czechoslovakia

Theresienstadt
Alhostice
Bohušovice
Kopisti
Litoměřice
Litoměřice-Radobylberg
Lovosice
Neštěmice
Stí
Terezín

Kratzau/Chrastava (sub-camp of **Gross-Rosen – Rogožnica**, Poland)

Belgium

Breendonk (no sub-camp known)

Czechoslovakia

Theresienstadt (9 sub-camps)

Estonia

Vaivara

Finland

Kangasjärvi
Kõveri

France

Argelès
Aurigny
Brens
Drancy Gurs
Le Vernet
Les Milles

Germany

Natzweiler-Struthof (70 sub-camps)
Asbach
Auerbach-Bensheim
Bad-Oppenau
Baden-Baden
Balingen
Bisingen
Dautmergen
Dormettingen
Erzingen
Frommern
Scherzingen
Schomberg
Wüste
Zepfenhan

Bernhausen
Bingau
Bischofsheim
Calw
Cernay
Cochem
Cochem Treis
Colmar
Darmstadt
Daudenzell
Dautmergen
Donauwiese
Echterdingen
Ellwangen
Ensingen
Frankfurt am Main
Frommern
Geisenheim
Geislingen
Goben
Gross-Sachsenheim
Güttenbach
Hailfingen
Haslach
Heilbronn
Heppenheim
Hessenthal
IffezheimIffezheim – Baden Oos-Sandweiller
Kaisheim
Kochendorf
Leonberg
Longwy-Thiel
Mannheim
Metz
Mosbach
Neckarelz I and II
Neckarelz Bad Rappenau
Neckargartach-Heilbronn
Neckargerach
Neckargerach Unterschwarsach
Neunkirchen
Oberehnheim-Obernai
Obrigheim
Peltre
Plattenwald
Rothau
Saint-Die
Sainte Marie aux Mines

Sandweier
Sanhofen
Schirmeck
Schönberg
Schörzingen
Schwabisch-Hall
Spaichingen
Tailfingen
Urbes Wesserling
Vaihingen-Enz
Vaihingen/Unterriexingen
Wasserralfingen
Weckrieden
Wasserling
Zuffenhausen

Noé
Récébédou
Rieucros
Rivesaltes
Suresnes
Thil

North Africa

Abadla
Ain el-Ourak
Béchar
Berguent
Bogari
Bouarfa
Djelfa
Kénadsa
Méridja
Missour
Tendrara

Holland

Amersfoort

Ommen

Vught (12 sub-camps)
Arnhem
Breda
Eindhoven
Gilze en Rijen
's-Gravenhage (The Hague)
Haaren par Tilburg
Leeuwarden
Moerdijk
Rozendaal
Sint-Michielsgestel
Valkenburg par Leiden
Venlo

Westerbork (transit camp)

Italy

Bolzano
Fossoli
Risiera di San Sabba (no sub-camp known)

Latvia

Dundaga
Eleje-Meitenes
Jungfernhof
Lenta
Riga
Riga-Kaiserwald
Spilve

Lithuania

Aleksotaskowno
Kaunas
Palemonas
Pravieniškės
Volary

Norway

Bærum
Berg
Bredtvet
Falstadt
Tromsdalen
Ulven

Poland

Auschwitz-Birkenau (extermination camp – 51 sub-camps)
Altdorf/Stara Wieś
Althammer/Stara Kuźnia
Babice
Bauzug
Beruna
Bismarckhütte/Chorzów Batory
Blechhammer/Sławięcice
Bobrek/Oścwięcim
Brunn/Brno
Budy
Charlottegrube/Rydułtowy
Chełmek/Chełmek-Paprotnik
Chorzów
Chrzanów
Czernica
Eintrachthütte/Świętochłowice
Ernforst
Ernfort-Sławęcice
Freudenthal/Bruntál
Fürstengrube/Laski
Gleiwitz I, II, II, IV/Gliwice
Golleschau/Goleszów
Gunthergrubbe/Ledziny
Harmęże
Hindenburg/Zabrze
Hubertushütte-Hohenlinde/Łagiewniki
Janigagrube-Hoffnung/Libiąż
Jawischowitz
Kobio/Kobiór
Lagischa/ŁagiszaLaurahütte/Siemianowice
Lepziny-Lawki
Lesslau-Włocławek
Libiąż Mały
Łuków
Monowitz/Monowice
Mysłowice
Neu Dachs/Jaworzno
Neustadt/Prudnik
Pławy
Rajsko

Rybnik
Rydułtowy
Siemianowice
Sosnowitz I and II/Sosnowiec
Trzebinia
Tscechwitz/Czechowice
Włocławek/Leslau
Zasole
Zittau

Belzec (extermination camp – 1 sub-camp)
Izbica
Bierznow
Biesiadka
Dzierżązna & Litzmannstadt

Gross-Rosen – Rogoźnica (77 sub-camps)
Aslau
Bad Warmbrunn/Cieplice
Bautzen
Berndorf/Bernartice
Blechhammer
Bolkenhain/Bolków
Breslau/Wrocław
Brief/Brzeg
Brünnlitz/Brněnec
Brusay/Brzezowa
Buchwald Höhenwöse
Bunzlau/Bolesławiec
Bunzlau-Rauscha/Ruszów
Christianstadt
Dornhau
Dyhernfurth/Brzeg Dolny
Erlenbusch
Eule
Falkenberg
Faulbruk
Frierland
Fürstenstein
Gabersdorf
Gassen
Gebhardsdorf/Giebułtów
Gellenau/Jeleniów
Görlitz
Graben
Granefort
Grulich/Králíky
Grünberg
Gruschwitz/Kruszwica
Halbstadt/Meziměstí
Hartmannsdorf
Hirschberg/Jelenia Góra
Hohenelbe/Vrchlabí
Kaltwasser
Kamenz
Kittlitztreben/Kotlicki-Trebin
Kurzbach Grunthal
Landeshut/Kamienogora
Langenbielau/Bielawa
L'Arche Ludwigsdorf
Lehmwasser
Leszno/Lissa
Mahrisch
Markstädt/Laskowice
Marzdorf/Martínkovice
Merzbachtal
Mittelsteine
Neisse-Neusalz Oder/Nowa Sól
Niesky
Niesky Klein
Niesky Wittischenau
Radisch
Oberalstadt
Oberwüstegiersdorf
Parschnitz/Porici
Peterswaldau
Prausnitz/Brusnica
Rauscha/Ruszów
Reichenau/Rzeszów
Reichenau Reichenbach
Reichenau Reichenberg Liberal
Schmiedeberg
Schotterwerk
Seuferwassergraben
Striegau/Strzegom
Tannhausen
Waldenburg
Weiswasser
Wolfsberg
Wustegierdorf/Giercze Puste
Wustegierdorf Station
Wüstewaltersdorf
Zittau

Czwartacki
Huta Komarowska
Janowska
Kraków
Kulmhof – **Chełmno** (extermination camp – no sub-camp known)
Lemberg
Lublin (prison – no sub-camp known)
Lwów (Lemberg)

Majdanek (extermination camp – 3 sub-camps)
Budzyń
Hrubieszów
Lublin

Mielec
Pawiak (prison – no sub-camp known)
Płaszów (work camp, later a sub-camp of **Majdanek**)
Poniatowa
Pustków
Radogoszcz
Radom
Schmolz/Smolec
Schokken/Skoki
Sobibor

Stutthof – Sztutowo (40 sub-camps)
Bocień
Bromberg
Brusy
Chorabie
Cieszyny
Danzig-Burggraben/Kokoszki
Danzig-Neufahrwasser

Danzigerwerf/Gdańsk
Dzimianen
Elbing/Elbląg
Gdynia
Gendorf
Gerdenau
Graudenz
Grodno
Gutowo
Gwiździny
Heiligenbeil
Jessu
Kokoschken
Kolkau
Krzemieniewo
Lauenburg
Malken Mierzynek
Nawitz
Niskie
Obrzycko
Prault
Pruszcz
Rosenberg/Brodnica
Scherokopas
Schiffenbeil
Serappen
Sophienwalde
Slipsk
Stargorod
Szczecin/StettinToruń

Treblinka
Wieliczka
Żabikowo (work camp – no sub-camp known)
Zakopane

Russia

Akmétchetka
Bar
Baranówka
Bisjumujsje
Bogdanovka
'Citadelle'
Czwartacki
Daugavpils
Domanivka
Edineti
Khorol
Kielbasin (or **Kelbassino**)
Klooga
Lemberg
Mežaparks
Ponary
Rawa Ruska
Salaspils
Strazdumujsje
Vertigen
Yanowski (for all these camps, no sub-camp known)

Yugoslavia

Banjica
Bročice
Chabatz
Đakovo
Danica
Gornja Reka
Gradiška
Jadovno
Jasenovac
Jastrebarsko
Kragujevac
Krapje
Kruščica
Lepoglava
Loborgrad
Sajmište
Sisak
Slano
Slavonska-Požega
Stara Gradiška
Tašmajdan
Zemun

Appendix II

Most Populated Liberated/ Captured Concentration Camps and Death Camps

Camp: **Auschwitz**
Type: Concentration/Extermination
Location: Oświęcim, Poland (near Kraków)
Date: 26 May 1940
Evacuated: 18 January 1945
Liberated: 27 January 1945 by Soviets
Murdered: 1,100,000

Camp: **Belzec**
Type: Extermination
Location: Belzec, Poland
Date: 17 March 1942
Evacuated: –
Liberated: Liquidated by Nazis, December 1942
Murdered: 600,000

Camp: **Bergen-Belsen**
Type: Detention; Concentration (after March 1944)
Location: near Hanover, Germany
Date: April 1943
Evacuated: –
Liberated: 15 April 1945 by British
Murdered: 35,000

Camp: **Buchenwald**
Type: Concentration
Location: Buchenwald, Germany (near Weimar)
Date: 16 July 1937
Evacuated: 6 April 1945
Liberated: 11 April 1945 (self-liberated); 11 April 1945 by Americans
Murdered: unknown

Camp: **Chełmno**
Type: Extermination
Location: Chełmno, Poland
Date: 7 December 1941; 23 June 1944
Evacuated: –
Liberated: Closed March 1943 (but reopened); Liquidated by Nazis, July 1944
Murdered: 320,000

Camp: **Dachau**
Type: Concentration
Location: Dachau, Germany (near Munich)
Date: 22 March 1933
Evacuated: 26 April 1945
Liberated: 29 April 1945 by Americans
Murdered: 32,000

Camp: **Dora-Mittelbau**
Type: Sub-camp of Buchenwald; Concentration (after October 1944)
Location: near Nordhausen, Germany
Date: 27 August 1943
Evacuated: 1 April 1945
Liberated: 9 April 1945 by Americans
Murdered: unknown

Camp: **Drancy**
Type: Assembly/Detention
Location: Drancy, France (suburb of Paris)

Date: August 1941
Evacuated: –
Liberated: 17 August 1944 by Allied forces
Murdered: unknown

Camp: **Flossenbürg**
Type: Concentration
Location: Flossenbürg, Germany (near Nuremberg)
Date: 3 May 1938
Evacuated: 20 April 1945
Liberated: 23 April 1945 by Americans
Murdered: unknown

Camp: **Gross-Rosen**
Type: Sub-camp of Sachsenhausen; Concentration (after May 1941)
Location: near Wrocław, Poland
Date: August 1940
Evacuated: 13 February 1945
Liberated: 8 May 1945 by Soviets
Murdered: 40,000

Camp: **Majdanek**
Type: Concentration/Extermination
Location: Lublin, Poland
Date: 16 February 1943
Evacuated: July 1944
Liberated: 22 July 1944 by Soviets
Murdered: 360,000

Camp: **Mauthausen**
Type: Concentration
Location: Mauthausen, Austria (near Linz)
Date: 8 August 1938
Evacuated: –
Liberated: 5 May 1945 by Americans
Murdered: 120,000

Camp: **Neuengamme**
Type: Sub-camp of Sachsenhausen; Concentration (after June 1940)
Location: Hamburg, Germany
Date: 13 December 1938
Evacuated: 29 April 1945
Liberated: May 1945 by British
Murdered: 56,000

Camp: **Płaszów**
Type: Concentration (after January 1944)
Location: Kraków, Poland
Date: October 1942
Evacuated: Summer 1944
Liberated: 15 January 1945 by Soviets
Murdered: 8,000

Camp: **Ravensbrück**
Type: Concentration
Location: near Berlin, Germany
Date: 15 May 1939
Evacuated: 23 April 1945
Liberated: 30 April 1945 by Soviets
Murdered: unknown

Camp: **Sachsenhausen**
Type: Concentration
Location: Berlin, Germany
Date: July 1936
Evacuated: March 1945
Liberated: 27 April 1945 by Soviets
Murdered: unknown

Camp: **Sered'**
Type: Concentration
Location: Sered', Slovakia (near Bratislava)
Date: 1941/42
Evacuated: –
Liberated: 1 April 1945 by Soviets
Murdered: unknown

Camp: **Sobibor**
Type: Extermination
Location: Sobibor, Poland (near Lublin)
Date: March 1942
Evacuated: Revolt on 14 October 1943; Liquidated by Nazis, October 1943
Liberated: Summer 1944 by Soviets
Murdered: 250,000

Camp: **Stutthof**
Type: Concentration (after January 1942)
Location: near Danzig, Poland
Date: 2 September 1939
Evacuated: 25 January 1945

Liberated: 9 May 1945 by Soviets
Murdered: 65,000

Camp: **Theresienstadt**
Type: Concentration
Location: Terezín, Czech Republic (near Prague)
Date: 24 November 1941
Evacuated: Handed over to Red Cross, 3 May 1945
Liberated: 8 May 1945 by Soviets
Murdered: 33,000

Camp: **Treblinka**
Type: Extermination
Location: Treblinka, Poland (near Warsaw)
Date: 23 July 1942
Evacuated: Revolt on 2 April 1943; Liquidated by the SS, April 1943
Liberated: –
Murdered: 800,000

Camp: **Westerbork**
Type: Transit
Location: Westerbork, Netherlands
Date: October 1939
Evacuated: –
Liberated: 12 April 1945; camp handed over to Kurt Schlesinger
Murdered: unknown